Muddy Water to Dry Land

Muddy Water to Dry Land

A Seven-Step Journey to Improve Your Personal and Interpersonal Skills

Marie McCurley

TKK Publishers
La Grange Park, Illinois

© 2014 Marie McCurley

All rights reserved. No part of this book may be reproduced or transmitted in any form or by any means, electronic or mechanical, including photocopying, recording, or by an information storage and retrieval system without permission in writing from the publisher.

ISBN 9780967020013

Library of Congress Control Number: 2014921996

This book was printed in the United States of America

DISCLAIMER

The purpose of this book is to give general information. This information is not presented by a medical practitioner and is for informational purposes only. Neither author nor publisher shall have any responsibility or liability to any person or entity with respect to loss or harm allegedly caused directly or indirectly by the information contained in this book. This book is a work of the author's experience, opinion, and research. Names, characters, places and incidents are used fictitiously. Any resemblances to actual persons, living or dead, or to actual events or locales are entirely coincidental.

Other published books:

The Easy Way to Plan a Church Conference

Copyright 2000, Revised Edition 2013 by Marie McCurley

ISBN 096702000X, ISBN 9780615617886

www.tkkpublishers.com

Dedication

This book is dedicated to the memory of my parents, who were instrumental in shaping my values and my two sons whose lives were cut short. I also dedicate this book to my children (Tanya, Kim, and Kevin) who support me without question in all my endeavors. I want my grandchildren (Latesha, Angela, Jermaine, Keith, Rashaad, Kayla, and Kameron) to know that all things are possible.

"Yes, it is true that opportunity comes only once to your door. But, since it comes at birth and stays throughout life, You can grasp its hand at any moment, and bid it enter!"

—LANDONE

Table of Contents

Preface 11

Acknowledgements 15

Introduction 17

Step 1: Enhance Your Self-Esteem 21

Step 2: Communicate Clearly 41

Step 3: Manage Conflict 59

Step 4: Exhibit Integrity 77

Step 5: Deal With Betrayal 99

Step 6: Cope With the Loss of a Loved One .115

Step 7: Be Persistent 129

Bonus Article: The Habit of Happiness 141

About the Author 157

Bibliography 159

Preface

I wrote this book as a result of a painful experience at a young age and that experience was instrumental in the way I live my life. I want to share some skills and techniques that may help you get through a few of life's challenges. From my initial thought, it was about five years before I actually began to write this book. The content of this book comes from my experiences and my research.

There are many ways to express being in muddy water. Down through the years many of you may have said or may have heard a few of the following expressions: in a Catch 22, things are going haywire, going through the mill, left high and dry, in dire straits, in over my head, reached a stumbling block, in an uphill battle, and if it wasn't for bad luck, I wouldn't have any luck at all. Despite the hopeless feeling that we have when we use the above expressions, there are ways to deal with these challenges.

My first encounter with what I call muddy water was at the tender age of six. There were eight children in my family and I never thought of my upbringing as living in hard times. My father worked and my mother was the homemaker. There was always a roof over our head and food to eat. If my family needed, beans, rice, spices, bread, money, or whatever, my mother borrowed it from one of the neighbors and paid it back when she could—maybe. I was a young adult when I learned there was a name for my family situation. The name was *poor*.

As a child, I loved to play hopscotch and jump rope. These two activities were my hobbies. Anytime that my mother let me play outside, this was my thing—playing hopscotch and jumping rope. Because of these two intensive activities, I quickly wore holes in the soles of my shoes. When a hole appeared, I would get a heavy piece of cardboard and put it in my shoe to cover the holes. When I got a hole in the cardboard, I immediately placed another piece of cardboard in the shoe. This process continued until someone gave me some shoes that fit or my parents had extra money to buy a new pair.

I didn't think anything of this process. I thought we really had a good life. It wasn't until I began first grade and had to leave my block that I had a rude awakening. When I began school, I was a happy go lucky girl. I felt secure and loved by my family and everyone on the block.

Well, happiness soon turned to misery and pain. At that time, when you were in the first grade and didn't have gym shoes to play in the gymnasium, you could take your shoes off and play in your socks. The janitor didn't want you to play in your street shoes and scuff up the gymnasium floor. That floor was always shining like a new penny. When I took my shoes off to play, I put them in the coatroom beside my classmates' shoes. There were others that had to play in their socks, too.

When the gym class was over, and I started to adjust my cardboard inserts in my shoes, one of my classmates started to chant "oooh you have holes in your shoes, you have holes in your shoes." Other children started to point and laugh. I felt really hurt. The tears welled up in my eyes but I refused to let them fall. At that moment I realized that having holes in your shoes was not normal for every child.

I went home that day feeling hurt and humiliated. When I entered the door to my home, I emphatically told my mother that I didn't ever want to go back to school. My mother put her hands on her hips and said, "What happened?" I hurried and told her about the painful experience. With emotion in her voice and using a tone that I had never heard before, she said, "If you go to school, learn to read, write, and speak clearly, you will be able to do anything you want in life and no one will care whether or not you have holes in your shoes."

So at the tender age of six, I began developing a desire to do well in any situation. I heeded my mother's advice and began my journey from Muddy Water to Dry Land. Still traveling!

—Author

Acknowledgements

I acknowledge Rev. Marvin E. Wiley, Pastor of the Rock of Ages Baptist Church in Maywood, Illinois. His preaching and teaching were influential in inspiring me to begin my writing career.

Kathereen Henderson (Petie), best friend through thick and thin.

Rhonda Sculfield, a loyal friend who always provides me with impartial opinions.

I also acknowledge all those who were supportive in my personal development. There are too many to name but you know who you are.

Introduction

This book will give you seven steps to improve your personal and interpersonal skills. It was created to give you information, guidance, and inspiration. I want to make it clear that I am not a psychologist, doctor, counselor, or a life coach. I am a woman who has experienced some successes and many challenges in life.

I have written this book to share some of my responses to the challenges I have faced and to share some of my research on various topics. This book is for adults but can be shared with youth of appropriate age.

The process of self-development is ongoing. From the minute we are born self development begins. During our developmental stages, we are influenced by parents, teachers, caregivers and others who have constant interaction with us.

When we become adults, the responsibility becomes ours to learn skills that allow us to interact with others effectively. For this reason, we should continuously strive to improve ourselves and our interpersonal skills in order to get the cooperation and respect from others.

It is always a plus to be able to adapt your style to interact with other personalities. People are just people whether they are at home, in the workplace, in the nightclub, in the community, or in the church. People all have different philosophies and occasionally disagree on certain ideas or topics. It is during times of disagreement that you need to use certain skills in order to maintain civility. I'm going to share with you seven skills that I have used on my journey. These skills may help you keep your poise, respect, and maybe even a friend.

Step one in this book is Enhance Your Self-Esteem. In this chapter I will discuss what self esteem is and how to determine if you have low self esteem. I will also provide skills that you can use to raise your self esteem.

Step two is Communicate Clearly. This chapter will show you the importance of using tone, body language, and listening skills to communicate effectively with others.

Step three is Manage Conflict. In this chapter, you will discover just how easy it is to manage conflict with family, co-workers, friends, and within a group setting.

Step four is Exhibit Integrity. This chapter explores the importance of integrity in both your personal and professional life. It includes steps you can use to develop your integrity. You will also learn about benefits that you can enjoy if you make the effort to develop integrity.

Step five is Deal With Betrayal. Have you ever been betrayed? If so, you will be glad to know that you can overcome the broken trust and start a process to forgive your betrayer.

Step six is Cope with the Loss of a Loved One. Very few occurrences in life are more devastating than losing someone you love. This chapter will discuss the five stages of grieving and how to move forward without forgetting.

Step seven is Be Persistent. When you get off track and feel like you are not improving in whatever skill you are trying to acquire or improve, there are steps that you can take to get back on track.

Remember, the steps in this book are only recommendations to be added to the skills you already have. All of these steps will not appeal to everyone. Decide which steps you can use and file the others.

Step 1
Enhance Your Self-Esteem

Just what does self-esteem mean to you? Does it mean accepting yourself just as you are? Does it mean accepting credit for the good things you do? Does it mean that you can turn challenges and perceived failures into victories? Feeling good about yourself comes from within. It's important to not let comments and opinions from others dictate how you feel about yourself.

If you didn't read the Preface in this book, you might want to stop, go back, and read it now. It was so difficult going to school every day knowing that all the children knew that I had holes in my shoes. Even though my mother had told me what to do, it was not easy. My self esteem was dragging the ground. Therefore, I think this step is one of the most important steps in your journey.

Building your self-esteem requires evaluating whether you have high or low self-esteem, using a positive mental attitude, clearing your thinking, overcoming doubt and being creative.

One way to enhance your self-esteem is to know your self-worth. No, realizing your self worth has nothing to do with your bank account balance. It is about you, the person you are in life. We give others respect, love and consideration—but how often do we give ourselves what is due?

How you value yourself is based on the self-esteem you have. Healthy self-esteem leads to independence, happiness, and flexibility. It also increases the ability to adapt easily to change and create a positive outlook on any situation. Unhealthy or low self-esteem periodically leads to irrational thoughts, unhappiness, fear of the new, defensiveness, and a negative outlook on life in general.

How we see ourselves has a lot to do with how others see us. If we are happy, smiling and full of confidence, then others see us as someone they want to be around. If we respect ourselves and portray this, others will respect us. Even those that are envious of you may not like you but they will usually respect you. So, finding and developing your self-worth is all about developing your self-esteem.

Low self-esteem

If you have problems with low self-esteem, then you will follow a certain pattern in your thoughts and ways. You may occasionally see the following traits in yourself:

- You lack belief in yourself and are very insecure.

- You have problems showing and accepting intimacy in relationships.

- You never let your true feelings show.

- You never recognize and give yourself credit for your accomplishments.

- You have the inability to forgive yourself or others.

- You resist change at every opportunity.

High self-esteem

If you have high self-esteem you will see certain traits in yourself. How you see yourself may not be how others see you.

Traits linked with a high self-esteem are:

- You feel secure about who you are and have confidence in your abilities.

- You allow yourself to show your true feelings to others.

- You don't have intimacy problems in relationships

- You are able to recognize and take pride in yourself for your achievements in life.

- You are easily able to forgive yourself for mistakes and also forgive others.

- You don't allow other people's opinion to define who you are.

- You don't allow your past to dominate your thoughts.

There are plenty of ways in which you can boost your self-esteem and move toward a positive and healthy outlook. Here are some tips for building your self-esteem:

- Make a decision to let the past go.

- Forgive everyone who had a negative impact on your life.

- View mistakes as learning opportunities.

- Aspire for accomplishments rather than for perfection. No one is perfect.

- Change the way you interact with others. Be flexible in various situations.

- Identify issues that you can change and those that you can't change.

- Take pride in your opinions and ideas and don't be afraid to voice them.

- Your opinions may be different from others but they are yours.

- Set goals in every area of your life (career, relationships, lifestyle, education, etc.).

- Set long term, clear goals to get where you want to go.

- Set short term goals that are easily attainable and that will ultimately lead you to your long term goals.

- Repeat positive affirmations daily.

- Create a support group that will help to motivate you.

- Don't take other people's criticism to heart. Listen to what they are saying and determine if you can hear any value.

Use a Positive Mental Attitude Daily

A great way to build self-esteem is to use positive affirmations. Positive affirmations are simply phrases you repeat to yourself daily in an effort to change your mindset. Positive affirmations can change a person's outlook on life from negative to positive in just a short period of time. We can use our thoughts because they influence our feelings and therefore they can have a profound result on how we deal with life in general. By learning to control our affirmations and turn them into positive rather than being negative, you can begin to gain more control over every aspect of your life and make essential changes.

In my early years I did not know anything about affirmations. I just remembered what my mother told me and that was to read, write, and speak clearly. Because of that message, I accomplished a lot. Positive affirmations, I think, would have helped me accomplish more.

You can say positive affirmations throughout the day in order to establish a new thinking pattern. It is possible that you probably have established a pattern of negative thinking for many years and, if so, this will take time to overcome. In the beginning of your change, you can repeat positive affirmations many times throughout the day. This can be achieved by repeating positive statements quietly to yourself or out loud.

Positive affirmations can be used for many different aspects in your life. It can help you overcome difficult situations, gain more confidence in yourself, help you quit bad habits, or make changes to your life in general. I used many positive affirmations while writing this book.

Most inspirational books are judged by what you are inspired to do after reading the book. The information in this book was written to inspire you to work toward accomplishing whatever it is that you want in life. When you begin to use a positive mental attitude, a wonderful transformation begins to happen to you.

The following story is a very good example of a positive mental attitude:

> *A lesson learned from a child: There is a wonderful little story about a minister who, one Saturday morning, was trying to prepare his sermon under difficult conditions. His wife was out shopping. It was a rainy day and his young son was restless and bored, with nothing to do.*

Finally, in desperation, the minister picked up an old magazine and thumbed through it until he came to a large brightly colored picture. It showed a map of the world. He tore the page from the magazine, ripped it into little bits and threw the scraps all over the living room floor and then said, "Johnny, if you can put this all together, I'll give you a dollar". The minister thought this would take Johnny most of the morning. But within ten minutes there was a knock on his study door. It was his son with the completed puzzle.

The minister was amazed to see Johnny finished so soon, with the pieces of paper neatly arranged and the map of the world back in order. "Son, how did you get that done so fast?" the minister asked. "Oh," said Johnny, "it was easy. On the other side, there was a picture of a man. I just put a piece of paper on the bottom, put the picture of the man together, put a piece of paper on top, and then turned it over. I figured that if I got the man right, the world would be right." The minister smiled, and handed his son a dollar. "And you've given me my sermon for tomorrow," he said. "If a man is right, his world will be right."

There's a great lesson in this story. If you are unhappy with your world and want to change it, the place to start is with yourself. If you are right, your world will be right. When you have a positive mental attitude, the problems of your world tend to bow before you.

Clear Your Thinking

You are what you think. But what do you think? How orderly are your thought processes? How straight is your thinking? And how clean are your thoughts? There are certain mental cobwebs that clutter up the thinking of almost everyone, even the most brilliant minds. Some thoughts are negative feelings, emotions, passions, habits, beliefs, and prejudices. Our thoughts become entangled in these webs. Sometimes we have undesirable habits and we want to correct them. There are times when we are strongly tempted to do wrong. We do wrong and like an insect caught in a spider's web, we struggle to get free.

Our conscious will is in conflict with our imagination and the will of our subconscious mind. The more we struggle, the more we become entrapped. Almost like being in quicksand; the more we wiggle, the deeper we sink. Some people give up and experience the mental conflicts of a living hell. Others learn how to tap into and use the powers of the subconscious through the conscious mind, and in turn, they are victorious over their thoughts.

An insect may get caught in the spider's web and once trapped, it is unable to free itself. Unlike the insect, there is one thing over which each person has absolute, inherent control, and that is his or her mental attitude. We can avoid mental cobwebs. We can clear them. We can sweep them away as they begin to develop. We can free ourselves once we become entangled and we can remain free.

The person who goes through life optimistically with a positive attitude is better able to deal with life and the many challenges he or she may face. A positive person is able to bounce back and recover from problems or set-backs in all situations they may experience. The optimistic person will see the problem for what it is. It is nothing but a temporary set-back which can be overcome. Since thoughts can either be positive or negative and you can only have one thought in mind at any one time then choosing positive will keep your thoughts, feelings and actions optimistic. This leads to being a happier person who is able to achieve goals much easier.

Take time out for yourself. Celebrate and pride yourself on even the smallest achievements that you accomplish. When you devote all your time to working, trying to be perfect, and trying to keep up with the Joneses, you wear yourself down. When you are at your lowest, this is when you may begin to depend on substances like food, alcohol, or drugs to keep you going. These dependencies can cause long-term problems for you, your family, your peers, and eventually lower your self-esteem.

Sometimes our opinions of ourselves begin in early childhood. The way our parents interacted with us and the way our peers and teachers treated us frequently have long lasting effects on each of us. Fear, guilt, criticism, and resentment are sometimes used to promote good behavior but occasionally they have the opposite result and cause many to develop low self-esteem. I sometimes wonder if I would have been less confident if my mother had given me a negative answer when I told her about the *hole-in-shoe* incident that I described in the Preface of this book.

Be careful what you say to your children and what you say about other children. I heard a childhood television star say that when she was eight years old and playing on the set, she overheard an adult star say negative things about her. She admitted that throughout her childhood and even now as an adult the comment she heard still haunts her.

Overcome Doubt

Doubt creeps in when building self-esteem but you can overcome it. Overcoming doubt is easy, if you don't doubt it, of course. However, most of us entertain an element of doubt in our minds about being successful whenever we try something new. In fact, almost everyone is in some way plagued with doubt of some kind. Take technology, for example. Do you think all the technological advancements that have been achieved would have been possible without questioning the prevailing doubts at the beginning?

Suppose you want to start a business or write a book. Are you absolutely sure that it will succeed? There is always a little fear or doubt at the beginning. I had doubt when I began writing this book. Some of my concerns were choosing the right title, would I have enough content to complete it, and would anyone want to read it?

Despite your doubt, you cannot let it keep you from your ultimate goal. The reason is simple: you must be prepared to risk failure because it is important for overcoming doubt. Dive right in to whatever it is without making rash decisions. Create your plan, set your goals, and analyze all of the possible consequences of your situation. Use the skills you have to deal with the outcome, whatever it may be. This is the secret to conquering doubt. Have courage to fight it and you are sure to defeat it.

Belief is the enemy of doubt. Learn to think positively and believe in your ability to be successful. Remember that you will succeed if you think you will and you will fail if you think that, too.

Remember, thoughts can be self-fulfilling prophecies so don't think negatively. Don't pay attention to the people who discourage you, those who revel in planting doubts in you, and those who are maybe just jealous of your efforts. Try to associate with people whose thoughts and attitudes are positive and supportive.

You can have healthy doubt. Some amount of doubt can always be helpful in gaining wisdom or achieving progress in life. But when doubt becomes a cause for your hopelessness and inactivity or when it stands like an undefeatable task in your way to reach your destination, draw upon your faith. You have to strengthen your will to succeed at all costs and weaken doubt by all possible means, so that you will lead a life of fulfillment.

You may succeed because of your doubt or in spite of your doubt. Or, you may have to accept the inevitable and compromise with whatever worst case scenario presents itself. If this happens, just change course and rewrite your goals. Start fresh on your revised plan. Defeat doubt before it defeats you.

It took me a long time to begin this book, five years to be exact. I had many doubts before I began writing. After I had completed my outline, set my goals and began writing, it became a joyful experience. I could hardly wait from day to day to find out what thoughts would come to me. It was much easier than I initially thought. Now, I am looking forward to writing other books.

Failure will come but remember to try and try again. You probably won't be fortunate enough to go through life without ever experiencing failure. However, you must understand that it is part of life. Failure does not mean that you are a failure. It only means that you must put another plan in place. Don't let go of your commitment, no matter how upset you are by failure.

In fact, any setback should only prompt you to double your determination to make another attempt at reaching your goal. You may have to make many changes in your plans. Building your self-confidence and self-improvement is very important. Every step towards building self-esteem helps get rid of doubt and you will be back on track again.

It's never too late to build healthy, positive self-esteem. In some cases where the emotional hurt is deep or long lasting, it can require the help of a mental health professional, like a counselor or therapist. These experts can act as a guide and help people learn to love themselves and realize what's unique and special about them. Don't be afraid or ashamed to reach out for professional help if you need to.

Be Creative

1. **Stay Healthy.** In this fast paced busy world, free time is a rarity. So preparing meals is not **always** easy. Make sure you eat nourishing meals and not rely so much on unhealthy fast foods. Find an exercise plan that you enjoy and stick to it. Change it when you want to, but keep doing some sort of exercise. Get enough sleep. To keep your mind focused, do meditation or something you like to do to relax. I love to dance so my exercise is 30 minutes of dancing at least three days a week. Recently, I began to meditate.

2. **Explore New Things.** We do so many things without thinking about them. These things become our daily routines—mundane and boring. Try something new. It can be something as little as taking a different route to work or something like taking up a new class in something you have always wanted to learn. Two years after I retired, I started taking piano lessons. I really enjoy learning to play new songs.

   You can go back to school at any age. The technology today allows you to take advanced courses in most areas of study on the Internet. This can be done from the comfort of your home at any hour. I take my piano lessons from the Internet...I don't have to leave the house. If I have a sleepless night, I get up and play the piano. No, I don't disturb the neighbors because my digital piano has volume control.

3. **Start thinking like Curious George.** Ask yourself questions about everything you see, hear, and read. Why? How? What if? Find out the answers to your questions. You can also keep a curious journal and track all of your findings. I love the process of learning. You are never too old to learn.

4. **Read a new book.** Choose one that you wouldn't normally choose. Pick up a book at the library or go on the Internet. There are books that you can download to your computer, tablet or phone. If you can't find time to read, there are audio books that you can download and listen to while exercising or traveling. I am going to make an audio version of this book. If you have always preferred reading nonfiction, pick up a fiction book. There are so many interesting books to read and so many different genres to choose from.

5. **Act like a kid.** Children are so carefree, honest and enjoy fun things. Think about

what you used to do for fun as a child. Paint a picture; go to your local amusement park. Do anything that a kid would do. Take your children, or if you are a grandparent, take your grandchildren. Just have fun. I like to play table tennis with my grandchildren.

6. **Everyone needs a little me time.** Take time out for yourself every day. Sometimes we get so caught up in doing for everyone else that we forget about ourselves. It can be for a short period of time. Whatever it is you decide to do, just let it be for you.

7. **What if?** What if the end of the world was tomorrow? What if you did go to college? Make up your own what if questions and just see where your brain takes you.

8. **Never assume anything.** Assuming anything always gets someone in trouble. You might assume that the person who cut you off this morning was inconsiderate. What if they were rushing their child to the hospital and didn't even realize what happened?

9. **Write about you.** Who are you? What kind of person are you? Where have you been in your life? Why do you do the things the way you do? Do you have any established

goals you would like to achieve? How do you live your life each day?

10. **Have conversations with people.** Listen closely to what they have to say instead of waiting impatiently for your turn to speak. What would it be like to be this person? Imagine how they live and think. When I talk to people, I listen carefully to what they are saying and imagine what they didn't say. I listen to their tone and look at their facial expressions. When people are tooting their own horn (or should I say telling you some of the things that they have accomplished), just listen, don't try saying something to top them. You will have your turn to tell about your accomplishments later.

Developing your creative side helps to build self-esteem. Everyone can benefit from creativity in their lives. You can use creativity to help with work projects, goal setting, home and family management, and a whole lot more.

When you keep a positive mental attitude daily, clear your thinking, strive to overcome doubt, work on your creativity, or learn something new, you can begin to see noticeable changes within yourself. A new feeling of empowerment will come over you and if you reach out to others with love, care, and respect, in return, you will enhance your self-esteem. As your self-esteem begins to increase, you will feel better about yourself and begin to see the world in a whole new light.

Step 2
Communicate Clearly

What you communicate to others about your motives, ideas, desires, and morals determines the concept of your personality in the minds of others. However, what you say can sometimes come across different than what you mean to communicate. What others perceive can be determined from a combination of the ways in which you get your message across. This can include words, body language, tone, clarity of the message, and even your listening skills as you respond to what someone is saying back to you. Changing your attitude will also help you communicate clearly.

Remember that your success can depend upon communicating effectively with other people. If you have been attempting to succeed in communicating merely with word choice, you may have failed again and again, for words are less effective than tones, and tones are less effective than body language.

When interacting with others, you should express yourself clearly and honestly. Anyone listening to you should have no question as to what you mean. Being clear is not always easy; therefore, speaking precisely has to be practiced. Use words to express your ideas. Use tone to express your feeling. Use only body language to express motives. Remember these tips and chances are you will not be misunderstood.

Most of the time when you communicate, you use your eyes, tone, words and some sort of body language. You also communicate with the clothing you wear. Your overall appearance makes a profound statement. Another communication skill that is often overlooked and needs attention is listening.

Do you hear words, or do you really listen? Do you use a process of thinking or reasoning while listening to get the true meaning out of what is being said? Here is a breakdown of the above communication components:

Eyes

Where do you look when you are communicating with others? You should maintain good eye contact without staring at the other person. Don't look at the floor or over the person's shoulder. Don't roll your eyes if you disagree with another's words. People will notice if they see your eyes roll or your head move side to side while they are trying to communicate with you.

Remember that you disagree with what is being said, not with the person. During your next conversation, observe the eye contact made by others. Notice whether you feel intimidated or involved. Become aware of your eyes during communication. If you think you need to improve your eye contact skills, work on it. Habits can be changed with practice and perseverance.

Words

What words do you use to express your ideas or to make a point? Use simple words that project the clearest understanding of the subject. It is not necessary to demonstrate your big word vocabulary, and many people who do this come across as trying to impress people more than trying to communicate with them. Above all, do not use profanity. Using profanity to express yourself gives the impression that your vocabulary is very limited and you have to use fillers. Profanity can also shut down the lines of communication when others become offended by the words you use.

Words can provoke anger or words can soothe. Words are symbols. You will find that a one-word symbol can mean to you the sum total of a combination of countless ideas, concepts, and experiences, and the same can be true of the person you're talking to. You will also see the subconscious immediately communicates to the conscious mind through symbols. Through one word you can motivate others to act. When you say to another person "You can!" this is a suggestion. When you say to yourself "I can!" you motivate yourself by self-suggestion.

Choose words carefully. Remember, once words are out, you can't take them back. Poorly chosen words can really hurt sometimes, so it's better to err on the side of caution than to later regret what you said.

Tone

Some people fail because they do not know how to use the four means of communication effectively in persuading and convincing others to accept their word. At one time or another you have heard someone compliment someone else, however, due to their tone, the *compliment* is obviously insincere. The words themselves are complimentary but the tone tells a different story with the spiteful infliction of the tone. The people may talk for ten minutes (600 seconds) and the spiteful infliction of their voice may last only a second. Yet, many believe the one second of the tone, and discredit the 600 seconds of words. It can, and has, happened frequently. In fact, it has happened to most of us at one time or another. You know, someone will speak to you with words but their tone and body language indicate they wish the words had been different.

Do you have a soft quiet voice or a strong loud voice? Both types need to be adjusted. If your voice is soft and quiet, some people tend to not listen or think you are weak or unbelievable. If your voice is strong and loud, some people tend to think you are aggressive and domineering. An even toned voice, which people can hear, works best.

You should practice the speed and tone of your voice as often as you can. The tone you use while communicating is very important and may determine whether or not you get a favorable response. Make an audio tape of yourself speaking. Ask relatives or friends to give you feedback on your tone. Also, the next time you feel angry, make a conscious effort to keep your voice and tone natural.

Body Language

Of course, communication by body language is not limited solely to movement. There is body language from head to toe and posture which helps influence body language. No matter what phase of communication you consider, you find there are basically four means: (1) words, (2) tone, (3) body language and (4) listening. When one of these means conveys one idea and another means conveys a different impression, you can come across as contradictory and fail in communicating because you unintentionally destroy the other person's belief in what you are saying. For example, how someone could be saying yes with words while shaking their head no at the same time. If it doesn't result in their disbelief, you may be confusing them. They can end up trying to figure out whether the message is positive or negative while not even hearing the words.

Do you know what type of non-verbal messages you send with your body language? Do you know that body language often speaks louder than words? When I conducted training classes, I could tell the energy level of the class by their body language which included facial expressions and posture. Sometimes the audience was erect and alert and at other times, depending on the time of day and the meal they had consumed, they were slouched and inattentive. I projected my voice and tone according to the body language I observed.

Make sure your body language expresses the image you want to convey. Adjust your body language so that it shows enthusiasm and interest. If you read concern on the face of the person you are communicating with, reflect that feeling. Ask if it's something that you have said that is causing the body language that you are observing. This will give the other person a chance to tell you what has triggered the expression. Remember, your body language says a lot about you. That is why it is important to make sure your body language is positive.

Listening

Listening is key to all effective communication. Without the ability to listen effectively, messages are easily misunderstood—communication breaks down and the sender of the message can easily become frustrated or irritated.

Listening is *not* the same as hearing. Hearing refers to the sounds that you hear, whereas listening requires more than that. It requires focus. Listening means paying attention not only to the story, but how it is told, the use of language and voice, and how the other person uses his or her body. In other words, it means being aware of both verbal and non-verbal messages. Your ability to listen effectively depends on the degree to which you perceive and understand these messages.

It is common when listening to someone else speak to be formulating a reply while the other person is still talking. However, this means that we are not really listening to all that is being said. We are developing an answer or response based on what we think is going to be said.

Even good listeners are often guilty of critically evaluating what is being said before fully understanding the message the speaker is trying to communicate. The result is that assumptions are made and conclusions are reached about the speaker's meaning which might be inaccurate. This and other types of ineffective listening lead to misunderstandings and a breakdown in communication. Active listening not only means focusing fully on the speaker but also actively showing verbal and non-verbal signs of listening. Generally speakers want listeners to demonstrate 'active listening' by responding appropriately to what they are saying. Appropriate responses to listening can be both verbal and non-verbal.

Make an extra effort to keep body language to a minimum while you are listening. If you don't understand, clarify with the speaker at the appropriate time. Listeners should not be tempted to jump in with questions or comments every time there are a few seconds of silence. I have been guilty of jumping in with a question or a response when there was a pause. When I did that, the speaker's hand went up and I was told, "Let me finish please." Embarrasing!! Don't be afraid to ask the speaker to define or repeat what he or she has said. Summarize the thought in your own words to see if you got the message correctly.

Even if we are not formulating a response while listening, we may still be thinking of other things subconsciously. During a conversation, how often have thoughts such as "What am I going to have for dinner?", "Will I have time to finish that report?" or "I hope I am not late picking the kids up!" crossed your mind? At such times, we are distracted and not giving our full attention to what is being said. In other words, we are not actively listening to the speaker.

Common Barriers to Listening

There are many things that get in the way of listening and you should be aware of these barriers, many of which are bad habits. Barriers and bad habits to effective listening can include:

- **Trying to listen to more than one conversation at a time.** This includes having the television or radio on while attempting to listen to somebody talk, being on the phone with one person and talking to another person in the same room, and being distracted by some dominant noise in the immediate environment.

- **You find the communicator attractive or unattractive.** You pay more attention to how you feel about the communicator and their physical appearance than to what they are saying. Perhaps you simply don't like the speaker—you may mentally argue with the speaker and be fast to criticize, either verbally or in your head.

- **You are not interested** in the topic or issue being discussed and become bored.

- **Not focusing** and being easily distracted, fiddling with your hair, fingers, a pen, etc., or gazing out of the window, checking your text messages or focusing on objects other than the speaker.

- **Feeling unwell or tired**, hungry, thirsty or needing to use the toilet.

- **Identifying rather than empathizing**—understanding what you are hearing but not putting yourself in the shoes of the speaker. As most of us have a lot of internal self-dialogue, we spend a lot of time listening to our own thoughts and feelings. It can be difficult to switch the focus from 'I' or 'me' to 'them' or 'you'. Effective listening involves opening your mind to the views of others and attempting to feel empathetic.

- **Sympathizing rather than empathizing**—sympathy is not the same as empathy. You sympathize when you feel sorry for the experiences of another, while empathizing is to put yourself in the position of the other person.

- **You are prejudiced or biased** by race, gender, age, religion, accent, and/or past experiences.

- **You have preconceived ideas or bias**. Effective listening includes being open-minded to the ideas and opinions of others. This does not mean you have to agree but should listen and attempt to understand.

- **You make judgments**—thinking, for example, that a person is not very bright or is underqualified so there is no point listening to what they have to say.

- **Previous experiences**—we are all influenced by previous experiences in life. We tend to respond to people based on personal appearances, how initial introductions or welcomes were received, and/or previous interpersonal encounters. If we stereotype a person we become less objective and therefore less likely to listen effectively.

- **Preoccupation**—when we have a lot on our minds we can fail to listen to what is being said as we're too busy concentrating on what we're thinking about. This is particularly true when we feel stressed or worried about issues.

- **Having a closed mind**—we all have ideals and values that we believe to be correct and it can be difficult to listen to the views of others that contradict our own opinions. The key to effective listening and interpersonal skills is generally having the ability to have a truly open mind—to understand why others think about things differently than you and use this information to gain a better understanding of the speaker.

Non-Verbal Signs of Ineffective Listening

With all non-verbal signals a certain amount of error has to be expected. Generally, signs of inattention while listening include:

- **Lack of eye contact with the speaker**—listeners who are engaged with the speaker tend to give eye contact. Lack of eye contact can, however, also be a sign of shyness or even insecurity.

- **An inappropriate posture**—slouched, leaning back or 'swinging' on a chair, leaning forward onto a desk or table and/or a constantly shifting posture. People who are paying attention tend to lean slightly towards the speaker.

- **Being distracted**—fidgeting, doodling, looking at a watch, replying to a text message, and yawning.

- **Inappropriate expressions and lack of head nods**—often when a listener is engaged with a speaker they nod their head, this is usually an almost subconscious way of encouraging the speaker and showing attention. Lack of head nods can mean the opposite—listening is not happening. The same can be true of facial expressions; attentive listeners use smiles as feedback mechanisms and to show attention.

When you listen, learn to reflect the speaker's feeling when you are confirming what has been said. To listen carefully means to take all components into consideration such as voice, tone, words, eye contact, and body language. If you truly listen, you will make the proper response.

Active listening is a key interpersonal skill and a prerequisite to many other communication skills. It can take time and practice to learn to do it effectively. But by learning to listen more effectively, anyone can improve the quality of their professional and personal life. Active listening shows you are concerned and care about what the other person is saying.

Clear communication can help in all types of relationships. From talking with your boss at work to effectively communicating to your subordinates, getting your thoughts and ideas across explicitly will help to enable work related issues and tasks to proceed more effectively.

These skills can also work wonders in the home, especially with spouses. When a spouse feels they aren't truly being heard, it can cause hurt feelings and frustration, which can often turn to anger. Clear communication is also paramount for children. When kids know *exactly* what is expected of them and there are no 'grey' lines, they are able to make better decisions and also realize there may be consequences if they don't follow the rules. This alone can help the parent/child relationship from a young age through the teen years.

While it can take time to perfect clear communication, it is well worth the effort. When people understand exactly what you're saying, there is no confusion. This clarity can come across as a person being comfortable with what they are saying, which in turn can come across as a form of assertiveness. Being assertive isn't a bad thing. It is often interpreted as confidence or being self-assured, which many people respect.

There is no certain time frame in which you can change how you communicate because it all depends on the individual. If you've found you're being misunderstood at work and/or at home, it may be time to seriously think about your communication skills and how often you should be practicing them. This isn't something that others will know you're doing, so you don't have to worry about what someone else might think. You can do it consciously whenever you're talking with someone. You can even have 'practice' conversations in your head or out loud to yourself if you want a little practice before using these skills in a real conversation.

Adjust Your Attitude

In order to communicate clearly, you may need to adjust your attitude, if needed. There are many factors that determine our attitudes. Our families, teachers, social environment, careers, life experiences, and religious beliefs are just a few things that help form our attitudes. Attitudes are also the results of successes, failures, and the way people have reacted to us in the past. Attitudes can change depending on what's going on in our lives at a particular time.

Some of us have health, financial, relationship, and other problems that have an impact on the way we communicate with others. If we are told that we have a bad attitude, we should find out what message we are sending and make an effort to adjust it. Many times we are not aware that we are acting in a negative way.

Ways to adjust your attitude

- Put aside your need to control and be liked.
- Set goals and do things to elevate your self-esteem.
- Don't focus on your problems.
- Develop a plan and take steps to solve your problems.
- Try to be upbeat and cheerful. Try smiling often.
- Try to find the beauty in everything.
- Think of the good before the bad.
- Have a zest and love for life.
- Avoid negative words.

Take some time to write a brief, honest description of your image of yourself. Ask your relatives or friends if they agree with your description. If they don't agree, ask for their description. Don't become defensive and hostile if they don't agree with you. Evaluate their comments, decide what area you want to change and work on it.

The more you start practicing these communication skills, the sooner you will see results. The process may be quick if you pay attention closely all the time, or it may be gradual if you're not thinking about it all the time. This can easily happen when you get busy at work or home and have a million things to take care of.

However, as you slowly begin to pay attention to what you're saying and communicating with your body language, tone, clarity, and listening skills, you will begin to change how you communicate and you will start to do it automatically. You will turn yourself from an okay or poor communicator into a great communicator.

Step 3

Manage Conflict

There are many causes of conflict. We cannot escape conflict. When one or more persons are involved in any communication, action, etc., there is bound to be some conflict. Conflict can impede progress or cause destruction; however, it also has benefits. It can produce interest, arouse curiosity, and even strengthen relationships.

In its online dictionary, Merriam-Webster defines conflict as "a struggle for power, property" and "a strong disagreement between people, groups, etc., that results in often angry argument."

Managing conflict includes solving problems and dealing with difficult people. We all have had or will have conflict during our daily living. Conflict begins early in life when toddlers and parents have conflict about eating and sleeping hours. Children have conflict with each other while engaging in play. Teenagers have conflict with parents regarding chores, curfews, dating, friends, and other things that influence their lives. Parents have conflict regarding children, finances, parenting, etc. Teachers have conflict with students regarding homework and class behavior. There can also be conflict between a supervisor and employee.

Let's examine a few conflicts:

A disagreement over where to spend Thanksgiving.

A husband and wife arguing over finances.

A clash about the details of a group report at the office.

A long-standing grievance over a friend being late for your get-togethers.

A dispute over a barking dog.

When you put people together in a home, a workplace, a friendship or a neighborhood, it seems natural that some sort of conflict will follow. After all, by nature, we humans like to get our own way and we can sometimes get a little unruly when we don't get it. Some sort of conflict in our lives may be unavoidable, but the stress that results from avoiding it or not handling it appropriately is avoidable.

So why do we often find ways to not deal with the conflict in our lives? Some of us may pretend a problem doesn't bother us, hoping it will go away. We try to handle the annoyance of the conflict rather than risk the personal fall-out that might occur if we confront it. The trouble is, by ignoring a source of conflict, we often make it worse.

Our bodies don't distinguish between physical and psychological threats, so when you are stressed over a conflict with a friend or co-worker, your body can react just as strongly as if you were facing an emergency situation. If you have a lot of conflict in your life, your body's emergency stress response is "on" most of the time. According to the American Psychological Association, long-term stress can cause serious health problems, including increased blood pressure, a suppressed immune system, increased risk of heart attack and stroke, and increased vulnerability to anxiety and depression.

Avoiding conflict resolution also can damage the important relationships we have with others. When handled effectively, however, conflicts can help us build stronger and healthier relationships. Let's look at the six steps we can take to better manage the conflicts in our lives:

1. Take time to assess the situation.

The first step in resolving a conflict is actually to take a step back. Don't respond in the heat of the moment when tempers might flare. This waiting period is especially important in terms of instant communication. Resist the urge to send off a snappy text or e-mail in anger. It's important to not air your dirty laundry on Facebook or other social media platforms either.

The old adage "let me sleep on it" can be helpful when you are faced with a conflict. Take the time to assess what is really bothering you. Decide if anything else could be a contributing factor to the way you are feeling: lack of sleep, an unrelated issue, or even a headache, for example. Sometimes just getting away from a situation affords you a clearer perspective of what is really going on. Ask yourself if there is a chance you might be overreacting?

After taking time to assess the situation, ask yourself what you want to accomplish. What outcome would you like to see happen if you address this conflict? If you can't answer this question, it may be best to wait to move forward with a resolution until you can answer it.

It's important to realize that in conflict resolution, the idea is not "to win" an argument but to come to a mutually agreeable solution to the problem.

2. Set up a time to talk, ideally face to face.

Okay, if it's the next day and you have a clearer, calmer view of the conflict, it's time to set up a meeting with the other person. Tell him or her very simply that you would like to get together to work on the issue at hand, which will only strengthen and/or restore your relationship.

Be specific about what is bothering you and share how much the resolution of the problem would mean to you. Unless you live in different locations, it's best to do this in person. Meeting face-to-face in a neutral location is preferable to talking on the phone or through online communication. When we meet in person, we can communicate more fully by picking up on each other's non-verbal cues in addition to verbal ones.

The way we hold our arms or sit on our chairs can reveal whether we are open or closed off. For example, a person with their arms crossed is giving the non-verbal clue that they are closed off and may be more difficult to talk with initially.

On the other hand, in person, we can nod affirmatively to what someone is saying and show our interest by keeping eye contact.

3. Listen to what the other person is saying.

So many conflicts could be resolved if we simply listened more than we talked. Ask the other person open-ended questions about the problem you are experiencing. There is a chance you both do not view the situation in the same way at all. By discussing it calmly, you will gain a new perspective that may help you get to a solution more quickly, a solution which can make both of you happy.

Research indicates that we only remember 25 to 50 percent of what we hear. No wonder we get into so many conflicts! Here's how you can practice active listening skills:

- focus on the speaker fully by limiting distractions (turn your phone off!) and use eye contact

- let the speaker complete his or her thoughts without interrupting

- provide feedback by responding with statements that begin with "I" not "You." For example, "I hear you saying that you are frustrated..." or "If I understand you correctly ..."

- ask questions to help clarify the situation rather than making assumptions such as "Would you tell me more about that?" or "How long have you felt this was going on?"

4. Take responsibility.

Validate what the other person has been saying about his or her feelings by taking responsibility for your part of the unresolved issue with statements such as:

"I really appreciate the time you are taking to talk with me about this," or "I am so glad we now have the opportunity to work this out."

Avoid the urge to bring up other issues. Sometimes we end up shooting ourselves in the proverbial foot by using the "kitchen sink" approach to conflict resolution. Don't throw a whole list of complaints at the other person. Stay in the present, and keep the conversation focused and specific to the current issue. Also watch the use of general terms such as "never" or "always" which can get in the way of finding a solution.

When faced with the other person's complaints, avoid the urge to keep quiet. Keep the conversation active or frustration and anger can set in. Be sure to acknowledge your shortcomings. Remember that a good sense of humor can help to diffuse your discomfort in this situation.

5. Brainstorm solutions.

Ask the other person how he or she would like to see the issue resolved. You may find after clearing the air, a workable plan is not far from your grasp. Perhaps you could make a list of possible solutions with ideas on how you could arrive at them. Be ready to give and to take in the spirit of compromise. Accept all ideas without judgment and think of ways to combine different parts of the suggestions to come up with mutually-agreeable solutions.

If you are not able to come up with an acceptable plan at this meeting, agree to take the time to think about it some more individually. Before you part, set up a time to get together again to review your ideas.

6. Move forward

Put the solution or steps to the solution into action. As you do so, let the problem go. Resist the urge to rehash the problem and instead move forward from a place of reconciliation. Many relationships suffer because one person moves on from a conflict while the other person never really lets it go and instead continues to harbor animosity or hurt feelings about it. Find a way to release those negative feelings so that you can forgive the other person and move on to establishing or re-establishing an open and healthy relationship.

Now that we've looked at the steps to resolving conflicts, let's see how we can apply them to real-life situations:

Family

There are probably no better people to push our buttons than our family members. We know each other so well, don't we? Here are a few of the family scenarios that can cause conflicts:

- a move to another home or to another city
- a separation or divorce
- a new job or the loss of a job
- a change in financial status
- a young person becoming an adult
- a birth or a death in the family
- a new marriage
- a disagreement about finances

As with all forms of conflict, the key to resolving family conflict flare-ups is through better communication. Let's look at how even a happy occasion such as a new marriage can cause strife. When a young adult gets married, some of his or her loyalties naturally shift to their new spouse. The new couple strives to create new traditions and customs, while incorporating some of those with which they grew up. All can be well and good until the holidays roll around.

Many families experience conflicts over the location of Thanksgiving dinner, for example. Mom and Dad can get hurt when their adult child announces plans to spend the day with his or her in-laws. Some parents will respond with "That's okay," even when their feelings are hurt. Tensions can mount if this conflict is not handled quickly.

By following the steps of conflict resolution, however, family members can come up with a compromise that honors both families. Here are some options:

- Spend Thanksgiving with one household and Christmas or New Year's Day with the other.

- Alternate years by spending Thanksgiving with one family one year and with the other family the next year.

- Meet all together as an extended family at a neutral location.

When it comes to arguments within a marriage, no other topic is argued about more than money. In order to keep this from becoming an issue in any marriage, it's important for both parties to be able to discuss how they feel about money. The way people act towards money is often learned in childhood and can have a great impact when those thought patterns are different than those of a spouse who may have been taught different views, or perhaps, no views at all.

When two people begin with a conversation to just explore their thoughts, it can lead to a deeper understanding of where each one is coming from. This can make it easier to discuss how money will be spent, how much should be budgeted for what, and even how much money each one can spend without having to consult the other person. Coming to an agreement doesn't mean the conversation is over for good. Money should be openly discussed especially whenever there is a change in the finances, such as can happen with a job loss or major purchase.

Workplace

Handling conflicts with co-workers or employers is probably the biggest source of workplace stress. According to a study by the University of Colorado Boulder, we typically respond to a workplace conflict by either avoiding it or battling it out. By working to resolve the problem, however, we can turn a potentially explosive – and job threatening situation – into a positive opportunity.

Let's say you and a colleague are assigned to present a report on a new sales campaign. You spend an entire weekend pouring over sales figures and expenses and then put together a PowerPoint presentation highlighting your results. On Monday morning, you're excited to show your co-worker what you have done. The conflict begins when she takes only about five minutes to glance over everything before poking holes in your report. At this point, your anger just about boils over.

In this scenario, step one of the resolution process is extremely important – taking the time to step away before saying something you will regret. Once you have thought the situation through carefully, you will be better able to respond in a constructive manner.

In a conversation that involves active listening, you may discover that your colleague felt undermined and/or threatened when you took the project home to work on it by yourself, so she acted defensively. Perhaps she would have preferred a joint meeting to go over the research finding before you put together a PowerPoint presentation. In addition, you both may have different work styles that appear to be at cross-purposes. One of you prefers to take your time on a project and work steadily while the other tends to make quick decisions. When you meet in the middle, you can find ways to combine your two styles to complete a successful report that uses each other's strengths.

Friends

Lack of communication often rears its ugly head in our relationships with friends. Sadly, many of us will sacrifice the friendship rather than deal with the source of the conflict. Let's look at a common source of conflict – being late. Some people are just habitually late. What they don't realize however, is how their tardiness can have an impact on others. Hurt feelings can arise when meals are ruined or other social events are missed because of the other person's lateness. Rather than being agitated about it or ending the friendship, this is a time to put conflict resolution strategies to work.

Your friend may not realize how his lateness is affecting you. When you calmly bring up the situation at a time you are both comfortable, you may be able to come up with a workable solution. Remember to use "I" statements rather than "You" statements. Here is an example:

> "I feel stressed about getting back to work on time when you are late for our lunch meeting," or "I really like to be in my seat for the start of a movie."

What could be a compromise in this situation? Perhaps the friend could phone you when he is on his way so you can leave at the same time? Maybe you could arrange to meet him at your office so you can keep working until he gets there? Whatever you work out, by talking about the problem and hearing both sides, you are halfway there to a solution.

Neighbors

Unwanted noise in the form of everything from dogs barking, lawn mowers and leaf blowers going, to loud music playing is a frequent source of conflict between neighbors. According to the U.S. Census Bureau, half of those Americans who moved between 2009 and 2010 did so because of the desire to live in a new or better home or apartment, and noise was the number one complaint they gave about their former home.

MARIE MCCURLEY

Many towns have noise pollution ordinances, but before you call the authorities and escalate the problem, try talking about your concerns with your neighbors first. Taking the first step of conflict resolution into consideration, you should wait until the next day to discuss a nighttime noise problem. Marching over there in the middle of the night can only serve to put your neighbor on the defensive.

After you have calmed down, visit your neighbor to address your concerns in a friendly, polite way. Frequently the offending neighbor has no idea the noise from his home is bothering you. By making him aware of the problem with "I" statements ("I have always been a light sleeper" or "I like to sleep with my windows open a little"), you open the way for a conversation instead of confrontation.

Areas of compromise can include anything from a mutually agreeable time for mowing or leaf blowing to the owner acknowledging that he needs to bring his dog in sooner at night. You can then use the conversation as an opportunity to discuss any interests or concerns you share about your neighborhood. Who knows? Maybe your neighbor will prove to be the person who can feed your cat while you are away for the weekend, and maybe you can bring in your neighbor's mail on occasion in return.

Conflict in Groups

Of course, there will be times in a group setting that your conflict will be with some difficult people. There are some people, that no matter what the conversation is about, will always find a way to distort or demean the issue or want to take full control of the conversation. When you are interacting with people who talk constantly, argue consistently, seek approval regularly, or blame others for everything negative that happens, there are some effective ways to deal with them.

Talks constantly

The person who talks constantly seems to know everything. This could be because the person is nervous and uncomfortable with silence. If there is a moment of silence, the person thinks they have to say something. When someone talks to the extent that others have little chance to contribute, calmly explain that others may have something to offer to the discussion. Thank him or her for the contribution and restate some of the important points that the person made. Try to make this person comfortable and not ashamed.

Argues consistently

The person who argues consistently may do so to get attention. He or she may have a mountain of personal problems and not know how to deal with them. They could be hurting inside and this action is a cover-up for them. When the person argues or becomes aggressive, you must remember to control your temper. Try to find some value in what has been said while encouraging the person to relax and think in a positive manner.

Seeks approval regularly

One of the reasons for someone always seeking approval could be that he or she has low self-esteem. They may have a need to be right. You must, if possible, avoid taking sides with this person. If it is in a group setting, encourage others to voice their opinions so there are several opinions on the table for discussion. When it is feasible, give suggestions on how to set goals and build high self-esteem to the entire group.

Always blaming others

Some people are uncomfortable with the fact that they make mistakes. They are usually afraid to take any kind of risk so when they blame or accuse others of negative communication, ask for the facts to back up the allegations. If you do this consistently, it may discourage this style of communication.

Chances are that you will eventually have to deal with a difficult person and using the above tactics will probably have a positive outcome with that person.

"When we take steps in our daily lives to get along with others, work out conflicts, listen when people speak, communicate respectfully, let go of anger, and respect differences, we affect the world in a positive way," says Naomi Drew in her book *Peaceful Parents, Peaceful Kids: Practical Ways to Build a Happy Home.*

Although avoiding conflict can seem to be the easy way out of a potentially explosive situation, it can serve to make the problem worse or cause it to resurface in a new form. When we actively seek to manage and/or resolve conflict when it occurs, we can create a more positive environment for everyone.

Step 4

Exhibit Integrity

You can't buy it, can't borrow it, and you can't take it. What is it? It is integrity. Integrity is an often misunderstood word. Most people have some idea of what integrity is but more often than not, they misinterpret it. The concept of integrity has become somewhat of a romantic notion, because it is widely believed that being an honest and good person is all it takes for you to have integrity. Yet, it is quite possible for loathsome people to have integrity as well.

Integrity means having congruency with your beliefs. In other words, you have to put your money where your mouth is. If your beliefs, values, and actions aren't aligned, you cannot have integrity. You have to act in accordance with your beliefs if you want to have integrity. From there on, anything you do will reflect that you have integrity.

Society expects you to have integrity, however, whether or not you develop it is totally up to you. This step will explore the importance of integrity in both your personal and professional life. You will also learn about the several benefits of integrity you can enjoy if you make the effort to develop it. In addition, a 7-step process for developing integrity is provided at the end of this step.

People who live their lives with integrity have gone on to achieve great things. Though there are some examples of people bending over backwards and making compromises for the sake of success. Their personal stories are examples of how hard it was for them to cope with the limelight. So, if you want to achieve your goals in life, you will need to show integrity.

If you want to develop integrity, all the information you require is provided in this chapter. It is up to you to read it from start to finish so you can make the most of it.

Do You Have Integrity?

Do you consider yourself a reliable person? Do people find it easy to trust you? Are you constantly asked to handle tasks that require a responsible person? The answer to these three questions will reveal whether or not you have integrity. Measuring self-integrity can be a dilemma for most people since their own perception of their integrity can vary from situation to situation.

There are some people who never accept that they are wrong, but someone with integrity would immediately acknowledge their mistake. Rather than blaming the problem on other factors or people, a person with integrity accepts and acknowledges the mistake was theirs. This attitude can make a huge difference and influence other people's perception of you. You will be considered decent, honest and reliable. In other words, a person with integrity.

Integrity is something others will look for in you. So, how do you analyze yourself to determine if you have integrity or not? Here are four factors to help in enabling you to assess your level of integrity:

Truthfulness

Are there situations where you are compelled to lie to get your way out of a hole? If the answer to this is no, it means you are a truthful person. Being honest means that you are open and responsible, two factors which are *extremely* crucial for developing integrity. So, if you don't feel the need to lie in most situations that arise, it means you are possibly a truthful person.

Accountability

Are you willing to accept your mistakes and bear the criticism for it? You might be surprised to know that most people would blame someone else for the mistakes they made. Often their excuses are not directed towards a particular person but a set of circumstances. Just ask yourself if you would trust a person who has an excuse for every situation. Of course not! So, if you are doing the same, you shouldn't expect anyone to trust you.

Ethics & Morality

Having a solid moral compass is important to stay on track. When lacking a tool to keep you on the right track, you might otherwise deviate. Therefore, it is best to define a moral code you are going to stick to. For this, it is crucial that your ethical guidelines are clear in your mind, or else you won't have a barometer to gauge your level of integrity. Make up your mind that there are some things that you will not do.

Respect

You have to show respect to others to prove yourself as a person with integrity. You cannot expect people to trust you and rely on you if you haven't proven yourself worthy of it. The last thing you need to do in this regard is look down on the people around you.

Below are four of the many factors that enable you to determine your integrity. Yet, they don't show a clear picture of what constitutes integrity. Here are some components of integrity:

Beliefs

Your personal beliefs are basically the values and ideals you believe in and act on. For instance, if you don't believe violence to be a bad thing, it is your choice. Yet, this personal belief of yours gives off the impression that you lack integrity. Therefore, your personal beliefs need to be such that they enable you to display integrity and follow the principles of integrity.

Values

Your values are an extension of your beliefs. It can be said that your values are the beliefs that you aren't afraid of showing to the world. Sticking to the example mentioned above, you may keep your preference for violence to yourself. On the other hand, you may choose to reveal it. It is revealing this belief to the world that will affect your integrity in the eyes of others.

Actions

Actions speak louder than words, and this is especially true with integrity. If you act according to your values, you will be viewed as a person with integrity. On the contrary, if you take actions that contradict what you say about your beliefs, no one is going to trust you. The bottom line is that you have to put your money where your mouth is, figuratively speaking.

Principles

Last, but not the least, are the ethical and moral principles you should be following. It is quite possible that your personal code of values and beliefs is not in line with what a person like you should be doing. Therefore, the principles play a major part in determining your integrity. If you are abiding by the principles, there is no doubt that you are a person of integrity.

These are the criteria you should be judging your integrity against. They will give you a clear idea of whether you have integrity or not.

Benefits of Integrity

One way to build your integrity is to start making small changes in your life. If you have been operating or living without integrity, you might be fearful of change, but if you want to grow, change is necessary. Building integrity may cost you in ways you never thought of. You may decide you don't want to wheel and deal in a specific circle of people anymore. You may lose friends, business associates, and sometimes become alienated from family members. Changing your life and building integrity will open doors because more people will learn to trust you.

A pertinent question that comes to mind is why should you make the effort to build and develop integrity. In today's day and age, hardly anyone has the time for self-improvement. The mere thought of freeing up your schedule so you can work on integrity could be perplexing. Why then should you make the necessary effort? This is where you need to understand the numerous benefits of integrity.

Respect & Admiration

The foremost benefit of integrity is that people view you with respect and admiration. If you feel the people around you don't treat you well, it is perhaps because you lack integrity. Therefore, if you develop integrity and start displaying it, you will earn the respect and admiration of others, which can lead to a stronger reputation. This will help you not only in your personal but professional life as well. Giving a good account of yourself is essential for earning opportunities for progress.

You Will Broaden Your Horizon

Integrity could be the key that opens the doors to numerous opportunities for you. If you feel your life has stagnated and you don't get any chances to make it better, it might be because people don't view you as a reliable and trustworthy person. Showing integrity enables you to broaden your horizon and make the most of the opportunities that come your way. This will particularly come in useful when you are applying for a better-paying job. Integrity is one of the major traits employers seek from applicants.

Feel Good About Yourself

There are a few tangible benefits of integrity. One thing you can hope for is getting a promotion at work. However, the intangible benefits are numerous, the most significant of them being you start feeling good about yourself. This is a feeling you can only enjoy once you experience it. If you have been feeling low and your self-worth has taken a hit, developing integrity may prove to be the perfect antidote to it. Your attitude and personality will also improve when you start feeling good about yourself.

These are just some of the benefits you get to enjoy when you have integrity. You will see for yourself how your life changes for the better when you live with integrity. It is well worth the effort you put in, without a doubt.

How Integrity Helps: Examples from the Real World

Rather than theorizing how important integrity is, it is important to look at some real world examples of integrity. In each of the following instances, it was integrity which helped salvage the situation. While the outcome might not be the desired one, displaying integrity at least delayed the inevitable. Let's look at some examples of how integrity helps from the real world:

CEO Turns around Business' Fortunes

Ever since the global recession took hold, many business' fortunes flipped over. Since they couldn't keep up with the downturn, most of them had to shut down. Same is the case with this business. Let's call it XYZ Co. for reference sake. XYZ, like most other companies, was struggling with cash flow and other such issues. Most businesses in similar situations choose to downsize, laying-off lower level employees right away.

However, the CEO of the company decided to display integrity instead of taking the usual route. He informed the employees about the company's problems. Moreover, he kept them up to date on a regular basis. As a result, the employees were fully aware of the problems at the company and willingly showed their cooperation. The CEO also shared with them his plan for turning around the company's fortunes.

When the situation worsened, the CEO did contemplate layoffs but instead asked the employees to take a 10% pay cut. Since he had been open with them from the beginning, the employees agreed and the worst-case scenario didn't materialize. So, not only did the employees take pay cuts but they also worked harder in an effort to keep the company afloat.

The result, you can guess; XYZ is back on its feet. While the profit levels aren't as high as they used to be, they are surely making their way there. If instead of showing integrity, the CEO had laid off a few employees, would this have been possible? Yes it could but the chances would have been slim. Through integrity, he revived his company's reputation and profitability.

Developer Develops Integrity

As is often the case in the service industry, the professional you hire patches together a workable solution. He does the job but it's nowhere near the level you were expecting. The worst part is that they don't even admit they are at fault. However, there are exceptions to this.

Dave had been working as a freelance web developer for several years. For one of his new projects, he had to work on software he was not familiar with. This was the first time he had come across that particular software and he knew it would take too much time for him to learn how to work on it. It would have been easy for him to find a similar program and get the project done. But Dave didn't want to risk his reputation. So, he simply came clean. He explained to the client what the problem was and why he could not do the project. He did lose out on a lucrative opportunity but the same client came back to him with a different project that was in keeping with what his style of work was. Dave knew there was a risk that the entire project could be cancelled if he worked on it just for the sake of the money involved.

Constructive Criticism

Some people criticize just for the sake of criticism. People with integrity criticize to help improve others. John, Paul, Richard and George work together in a large corporation. They are in the same department and often have to collaborate on projects. George's performance in the recent past had not been up to mark. The other three took notice and were discussing what to do.

John and Richard were pointing out the potential problems that were causing George's work to suffer. It was then that Paul walked in on the conversation. He listened to what the two had to say and proposed a solution: let's talk to George. Paul explained they could discuss the issue all day without finding a solution. Unless they talked to George about it, there was no way the situation could be improved.

As it turns out, George was going through some personal problems and couldn't find the support system to deal with it. By having the other three guys to talk to, not only was he able to vent his frustration, but also get back to the level of productivity he was at before. Though the other three were criticizing George, their criticism paid dividends when they showed integrity and talked to him about it. There are many similar examples where people displayed integrity and made the most of a situation.

A Test of Integrity

During my early career, I was an instructor at an agency that had the authority to test and certify clerical applicants for employment at various agencies. This authority allowed the instructor to certify that the prospective employee had passed the examination required. There was one incident where one of the prospective employees had applied for a promotion but did not have the qualifications to take the examination required. The manager at the hiring agency called me to ask if there was anything he could do that would encourage me to certify this particular employee. I told him no and that the employee should take the training necessary to qualify her to take the examination and return. At that point, I really did not think anything of the conversation.

During the following weeks, I received several calls asking what he could do to ensure the employee's successful passing of the examination. Each time I repeated that the employee should have the skills necessary to allow her to take the examination.

Later that year during the Christmas season, I got a call at my home from that same manager. I was annoyed that he was calling my home. The conversation went like this: "Our agency collects funds every year to donate to needy families and this year we wondered if your family could use the donations." Red flags jumped up everywhere. I realized that this man was trying to bribe me. I pretended that I did not know what was taking place and politely gave him the name and number of an agency in the community that accepted donations for needy families.

At that time, my family sure could have used whatever donations he had to give but my integrity was at risk. Making the wrong decision would have jeopardized my job and the agency that I worked for would have lost their ability to certify prospective employees. Needless to say, I never heard from him again. I have always been proud of that decision.

You must be careful from whom you accept favors because you can accept a favor and be forever indebted and perhaps damage your integrity. Accepting favors can impede your progress in many ways and keep you stagnant in your endeavors. You will notice others who began their journey after you did progressed at a faster pace...and now they are way up the ladder of success. You are progressing slowly because you accepted favors from people you thought were doing the favor for you; but in reality, they were only guaranteeing themselves a seat at the table. Those people will always remind you that you owe them a favor—verbally or by their mere presence. So, it is important to be careful when accepting favors.

Do you try to develop an image by wearing designer clothes, driving an expensive car or purchasing a home that you cannot afford? Your image is what your family and others think you are. Integrity is what you really are.

People like to put their confidence in people that appear to be credible. When people deem you credible, you have the ability to influence them. Integrity builds trust, has high influence value, facilitates high standards and results in a solid reputation, not just image. All of us know someone who is not the same on the outside as they are inside. Many people have worked harder on their images than on their integrity and are surprised when they are suddenly 'called out.' There are no shortcuts when it comes to integrity. In time, the truth will always come out.

It doesn't have to be something big; for example, often you will walk into the restroom and find that there is no toilet tissue. If you choose to bring it to the attention of the custodial staff, you show integrity. Of course, you can simply do nothing and just leave. It is up to you.

In most situations, there is little acknowledgement to be gained by showing integrity; but the people around you will admire and respect you and that will make it worth your while.

Steps to Developing Integrity

Before you can start developing integrity, you have to be certain that you lack it in the first place. To make it easier for you to understand, here are some things you can check to understand whether or not you lack integrity:

- **Do you constantly focus on yourself?** Is everything all about you? This is perhaps the most important of all factors you have to analyze. If you think about your best interests all the time, it could be that you lack integrity. Integrity stems from a sense of caring and thinking about other people. It may well be a personal thing but is influenced by others. So, if you don't care about the feelings of others and would trample them if the need arises, you definitely don't have integrity.

- **The opinions other people have of you have a huge impact on how you do things.** This is a sign that you are insecure and not confident in your abilities. Moreover, it shows that you care more about what people think than being a good person. It is common to see leaders changing their stance whenever the public opinion shifts. However, leaders who have integrity don't change their position regardless of what the people think. The reason is they are firmly grounded in their beliefs and values.

- **An inability to keep promises is another sign of a lack of integrity.** It is not just about fulfilling the promises you make to the people around you. If you fail to keep your word, it also shows that you lack integrity. Rather than proclaiming you will do something for someone, it is better to just do it. This way, you don't have to lose face and you retain your integrity. The best way to deal with this problem is to do more and promise less.

- **Do you look for the easiest way to get things done?** This is also a sign of a lack of integrity. People with integrity, especially leaders, don't look for shortcuts to success. They are intent on delivering what they promise without making any compromises. Any person who makes compromises regularly cannot have integrity. It doesn't matter that the compromise you make is personal or professional, it is a reflection of your character.

These are some clear-cut signs that a person may lack integrity. It is important that you analyze yourself objectively based on these points. If you feel you don't have any of these traits, it shows that you are a person with integrity. However, if the results aren't desirable, you can follow the seven steps listed below and develop integrity:

1. **Do You Need Integrity?** The first thing you have to do is answer this question although you have to bear in mind that integrity isn't for everyone. Integrity only matters to the people who have a place for it in their life. This is why it is crucial for you to figure out whether you need integrity or not, or else you would have a hard time putting in the required effort to develop it. Keep the benefits of integrity in mind when deliberating this question. Only then can you reach the correct answer.

2. **Be Honest with Yourself.** This is the step that is the most important. If you can start being honest with yourself, you will be honest with the people around you. Lying to yourself is much more dangerous and devastating than lying to others. More

often than not, the lies you tell yourself are far more significant than the ones you tell others. The problem is that your mind starts accepting those lies as facts and this is when it becomes a full-fledged problem. It is imperative that you start being honest with yourself. If you are incompetent at something and have been pretending to be an expert, it is time you come clean. You know yourself better than anyone does so only you will know the lies you have been telling yourself.

3. **Get Honest and Constructive Feedback.** Along with analyzing yourself and being honest about your faults, you should seek counsel from people who you trust and can rely on. There is a chance there may be some faults in you that you cannot see but others do. This is why it is crucial that you get honest and constructive feedback from people who hold some esteem in your eyes. You not only have to improve on your own but also in the way other people view you. Only then can you develop integrity.

4. **Focus on Improving Yourself, Not on Pleasing People.** As mentioned before, if you care too much about what other people think of you and you are constantly making an effort to win their approval,

you cannot practice self-improvement. You have to focus on improving yourself. You should keep in mind that becoming a better person would change the way people perceive you and your reputation will improve automatically when you develop integrity. Therefore, you should switch focusing from pleasing people to winning their admiration and respect by developing integrity.

5. **Make Stronger Decisions.** Developing integrity requires you to stop making compromises. Generally, people are forced to make compromises when they have to make an uncomfortable choice or decision. They try to find the easy way out and get the job done one way or another. This is something you have to avoid doing right away. You have to make stronger decisions. Success may be hard to come when you navigate the tough path but it is something you have to do to develop integrity. The next time you have to make a tough choice don't go for the easy way out.

6. **Call a Spade a Spade.** This is also something very important. You have to be truthful not just to yourself but to the people around you, since honesty is one of the pillars of integrity. If you cannot be

truthful, you cannot develop integrity. It is as simple as that. So, you have to start calling a spade a spade from now on. Be objective regardless of the situation. This means that you cannot backbite or gossip anymore, and don't make promises and claims you know you cannot fulfill. Most importantly, be honest about your expectations and capabilities.

7. **Set Some Time Apart for Yourself.** The last step of the process is to set some time apart for yourself. As mentioned above, hardly anyone has the time today for recreation. But the more you are surrounded by the people you know, the greater chance there is of a relapse. When you have worked so hard to develop integrity, it is your responsibility to ensure that you don't let go of it. It may sound selfish but it is important for you to break away from work and things at home and focus on personal growth. Do anything that stimulates your mind and makes you feel better about yourself.

These are the seven steps you have to complete to develop integrity. Keep in mind that you have to go from start to finish to be able to achieve integrity successfully. Make sure you don't quit midway as it would be another sign that you lack integrity. When you take the time to focus on improving yourself, you will begin to see results. This doesn't mean you won't have periods where you seem to regress. Just remember that you are a work in progress and, with time and attention to your thoughts and actions, you will soon be a person solidly grounded in integrity.

Step 5

Deal With Betrayal

Betrayal. The very word might send shivers of dread down your spine or cause the hairs on the back of your neck to stand up. It's one of those words people dread because it is a facet of life almost all of us experience, and many times we experience betrayal more than once. It is not like other dangers we encounter in our lives; we learn quickly not to pet strange dogs or they might bite us, or not to play with fire because it can burn us. Why then, does the human mind not learn to recognize and steer clear of those who would betray us? It is because betrayal never comes on its own; it is frequently linked to one or more other emotions, and sadly enough, the emotion betrayal attaches itself to the most, is love.

Betrayal by Friends

Let us first look at the idea of betrayal between friends. This is the first experience with betrayal many of us have in our lives, because we make friends at a very young age. Because of our early exposure to socialization, it is easy for us to learn to make quick, loving bonds within groups of friends. However, as early on as kindergarten, young children can experience betrayal when a friend or playmate turns against them, seemingly for no reason. This situation often repeats itself in friendships through adolescence and even into young adulthood. Let's examine the word betrayal in relation to friendships and see if we can learn how to forgive this type of betrayal.

Your best friend turns against you. Why? Is your friend your enemy now? Or has your friend repeated feelings you shared in confidence with a larger circle of friends? Have rumors been spread about you? Whatever the case may be, you are facing a situation where someone you once trusted can no longer be looked upon as a friend. Your heart is aching and your sense of trust is shattered. However, if at a young age you do not learn how to forgive this type of betrayal, you may start a pattern of mistrust in relationships that can have a negative effect on your entire life.

How can you start to heal after a friend betrays you? Don't look at the action of that one friend, but to your other friends, the ones who treat you well. These are the people who trust you, who are loyal to you, and who respect you as a person. Reflect on how those relationships enrich your life, rather than how this one friend attempted to damage your life. You must continue, regardless of how you have been hurt by a friend, to be a source of constant good companionship to your other friends. You have to be the friend you want to have, and then, good people will come into your life.

What you must try your very best not to do when a friend betrays you is make yourself the victim because the victim mentality will haunt you forever if you let it. It may hurt, but look inside yourself and examine this friendship betrayal from all angles. Has it happened to you before? Do you feel that you are a victim, that your friends take advantage of you? Has it occurred to you that your own way of behaving in a friendship may have something to do with that? Self evaluation can often lead to us understanding a facet of our own personality that may well be contributing to how others affect us negatively.

That statement is not a criticism; it is merely asking you to honestly evaluate whether or not you set yourself up to be the victim. Do you give your trust too easily to new friends? Do you confide in them too quickly? Although you might see yourself as open and honest, people who look to prey on others may see your openness as a chance to do some real damage. Think about your relationship with this person who betrayed you. Did you ever get a sense or feeling something was not quite right about the friendship? Don't ignore feelings like that. Did others ask you about this friendship or imply that it might hurt you in some way? Did the person who betrayed you have a reputation for discarding friends easily or quickly? If you saw one or more of these signs and still jumped right into the friendship with no hesitation, then perhaps you gave your trust a little too easily. Learn from it and don't allow it to happen again.

Now that you have examined your role in the friendship, it's time to take a look at the role of the betrayer. The sooner you learn to recognize signs of a person who will take your friendship and use it against you, the sooner you can stop being hurt. Did this friend ever give away a secret that you told before? If he or she did, how did you handle it the first time it happened? Did this person repeat gossip or rumors about another mutual friend to you? Did you listen in silence? If so, you encouraged this friend to act in a betraying manner and you should recognize that people who will repeat mean gossip *to* you are the same people who will gossip *about* you. Did this so-called friend have a reputation for being a liar? Did you catch them in lies at times, even harmless ones? If the person who hurt you displayed one or more of these signs, then you may have given your friendship away too easily. Recognize these signs and stay away from those who gossip, misrepresent others, or flat out lie. Sooner or later, they will do the same thing to you.

Can you forgive a friend who has betrayed you? You can, but that doesn't mean you ever have to forget it or to give that person your trust back. What you have to do in order to forgive is simple; put the hurt behind you and resolve in your mind that you will never hurt another person in that way. Understand the insecurity your betrayer must have inside him or herself, which causes them to hurt other people and understand that in order to be happy you do not have to harbor those types of insecurities. If a friend betrays you, it hurts. But, you can find it in your heart to forgive and to perhaps even reach out to your betrayer, once time has passed. Doing this can show you have forgiven them and give yourself some peace of mind. It can be a step for them too, in the learning process of how not to repeat the action.

Betrayal by a Spouse or Significant Other

As a child or a teenager, one may think the worst betrayal comes in the form of a friend betraying you. Unfortunately, as we get older, we learn this is not the case - betrayal in perhaps the worst form is when you are betrayed by your spouse, partner, or significant other. An intimate relationship, by its very nature, can almost send out an open invitation for betrayal because of how close the two people have become.

Think of your current or most recent relationship, whether it is with your husband, wife, boyfriend, or girlfriend. How much did that person know about you? More interestingly, what did they know about you they could use to hurt you? How could they be able to take your faith in them and your love for them and destroy it? If you have never been in a relationship where you have been betrayed, then hold on to your partner, because you have a keeper for sure. Betrayal within a relationship is painful, emotionally draining, and very hard to get over.

We enter into a relationship with the mindset the person we care about will be honest with us, trustworthy, and most importantly, faithful to us. This stands to reason, as in most relationships you are entering into an intimate relationship as well. So, the values of trust, faithfulness, and loyalty play an important role. If your significant other betrays you by entering into an intimate relationship with someone else, it can be truly devastating. It will have both internal and external affects on almost every aspect of your life. You will start to doubt your self worth, your attractiveness, and your ability to please your partner in an intimate way. Your life will somehow seem confusing and uncertain and you will question trust, both in others and within your own heart. There is no doubt that an intimate betrayal can be highly damaging.

If and when you are betrayed by your spouse or significant other, there are several steps you must take in order to be ready to forgive them. That does not mean you have to continue the relationship. But, just as with betrayal by a friend, if you do not forgive, at least within the confines of your own heart, then you will not be able to move on in the future and all your relationships will be tainted by this betrayal. When you learn of the betrayal, especially if it is a intimate betrayal, your first instinct might be to turn around and do the same thing to them. Don't do it; it helps no one, especially not you. So, do not lower your personal standards by having a fling. Instead, act in an adult manner and get ready to confront your partner.

Confrontation has to take place in this type of situation. It is only by confronting your betrayer and addressing the issues that you can grow and become better able to handle the situation. If you can confront the person there is less of a chance another person will try to push you around in the same manner. Don't yell and scream, however. That will achieve nothing and remember your goal is to forgive and move on. Be calm. Be clear. Be honest. Forgive in your heart and make a decision to decide as to whether or not you want to work on the relationship or end it.

Many people believe in second chances. I believe in second chances. However, we have to look at the old motto, "Once a cheater, always a cheater." People say it because it can be true in some cases. Can you really, truly, fully trust this person ever again? Or, will you spend the rest of your days checking his or her cell phone, reading text messages, and worrying yourself sick over a future betrayal? Most of us would do that but all of us deserve better than that. Once an intimate betrayal has occurred, the best thing can be forgiveness, although it can take time and consistency to recover from it.

If you truly love this person and want to stay in the relationship, this is the time to consider counseling. Professional counselors are trained to understand the many dynamics of relationships and can offer an ear to listen, advice, and most importantly, an unbiased viewpoint about what transpired. There are different approaches to therapy, and many people prefer to have independent sessions before merging into couples counseling, while others are ready for couples counseling right away. Do not allow friends and family to influence your decision.

Betrayal by a Co-Worker

Let's look now to the workplace. If betrayal by a friend hurts, and betrayal by a spouse is the worst emotionally, what can we say about betrayal in the workplace? Everyone should be aware that this type of betrayal has the potential to be the most damaging, because it can cost you your professional and ethical reputation, your job security and at times, even your career. Therefore, workplace betrayal is not ever to be taken lightly and we all need to be able to recognize the signs of it right away.

First, you must examine the situation if you feel you have been betrayed at work. Are you certain your co-worker acted in a vengeful or malicious way? What did they do? Did you not get credit for work that was yours? Before you fly off the handle, you need to find out if it was intentional or an accidental oversight. Did your coworker repeat confidential information? You have to ask yourself two questions in that instance: why were you sharing the information and was the other person really aware of the nature of the confidentiality?

Once you have determined that your co-worker intentionally betrayed you, then you need to speak with them. Notice the word used here is *speak*, not confront. Save confrontations for personal relationships. You cannot risk damaging this work relationship or risk damaging your reputation at work by having a big blow out with your co-worker. This does not mean you can't address the issue in a professional manner. Instead of accusing, ask, "Did you happen to mention...? Oh, you did. Well it was confidential." "Did you notice my name was not on that proposal? Can you tell me why?" Although it may seem you are giving the person a chance to give you an excuse, what you are really doing is demonstrating professionalism that is needed in this type of situation.

Since this betrayal has occurred in the workplace, the issue needs resolution. You cannot just walk away from this "relationship" unless you can walk away from your current job. So, what you have to do in order to make sure this does not occur again is to give the co-worker very crystal clear expectations. Do not mince words; be polite but firm. "Please check with me if you are unsure about our confidentiality policy." Try your best to let the situation cool off and do not dwell upon it. Most of the time, a work place betrayal is a harmless mistake and you will hopefully see that the co-worker can be trusted again. However, keep your eye on him or her for a while. If you see a pattern of betrayal emerging, you will know yourself, for your own benefit, this person cannot be trusted and should be treated professionally, but kept at a distance whenever possible.

Betrayal by a Sibling

This chapter could not be complete without taking a look at the world of sibling betrayal. This type of betrayal has its roots in childhood; who was the favored child, as perceived by the other child or children. Who had the new toys, the best college choice, the higher report card, the affection of mom or dad...it builds on and on and in a sibling relationship, if one sibling feels resentful and jealous his or her entire life, betrayal may be inevitable when the siblings are older. Of course, mixed in with sibling betrayal is often that mix of in-laws. Your sister marries someone you cannot stand. Your brother's wife hates you. Your wife dislikes your brother and sister. The intricate relationship amongst siblings is challenging at any time. Once you add the spouses or significant others into the equation, it becomes even more likely that jealousy or betrayal will occur.

Why, you ask? Because you have been told from a young age that you LIKE this other person. You love your brother. You love your sister. You were never given any chance to form your own opinions about your siblings nor them about you. So, when do those opinions start to form? When an adult sibling introduces his or her significant other into the mix and that person turns their eye on the siblings. All of a sudden, your brother who loves you barely speaks to you. Your sister who held your hand when you were little now has no time take your phone call. It goes on and on until all of a sudden, you are battling with each other like you did in the toy box when you were youngsters together.

How can you prevent this betrayal from occurring? First, by truly liking and befriending your adult siblings. Second, by agreeing with your spouse that siblings, like parents, are off limits when it comes to criticism or nit-picking. It might seem like a tough thing to agree to, but it will avoid future problems. Of course, you may ask, what if you agree to that but your brother or sister and their spouses do not? Well, you can only take the moral high ground for yourself and ask your partner to do the same. It works the same as the other betrayal situations work; when you are betrayed, do not look to fight back. Look to rise above and move on.

As for forgiveness, there should be no hesitation. This is your brother or your sister. They shared your parents, your childhood, and your earliest memories. They will be who you have when your parents are gone. You don't have to love their actions or love their spouses. You can maintain minimal contact if it is necessary. But, you do have to, in your heart, love them as unconditionally as you did when you were children together. The saying blood is thicker than water never ran truer than here. Forgive, continue to love, and keep the family peace.

And so, we have looked at the idea of betrayal from many possible angles. For the most part, as you can see, it is possible to forgive your betrayer and even learn from the experience. However, that is not to say it won't be painful, hard, and heartbreaking. That is why relationships, no matter what kind they are, are so fragile and should be approached carefully. Nothing can hurt a person as much as another person's cruel words or actions. Nobody can damage the soul of one person as thoroughly as another person can. Nobody can shake someone's self confidence or self worth as easily as someone you trust can. Your betrayers know you, you trusted them and they let you down. That is why it hurts so much and that is why it is so hard to get over.

Learning to Forgive

There is a word that is irrevocably linked to the word betrayal. At first, when we think of betrayal, the complete opposite of this word might enter our mind. However, it is nearly impossible to focus on the idea of betrayal without focusing on its counterpart—forgiveness. Why are these two concepts linked together, at least in theory? It's because when you are betrayed you are also being given a choice; to forgive your betrayer and use the betrayal as a learning and growing experience, or to hold back forgiveness and take the risk that you might not grow from the experience. Forgiveness is unique in that it has the ability to ease and soothe our own minds if we apply it to situations correctly. Forgiveness, when linked to betrayal does not always mean that the friendship, the relationship, or whatever it is can be patched up and can move forward. It can mean that one person forgives another, but trust is broken to the extent that moving forward is not possible.

Too frequently, when we humans are hurt, our tendency is to link the idea of forgiveness to the idea of forgetting. What we each must remember in our hearts is that it is possible to forgive but not to forget. Each of us has to ascertain if we can truly put a specific betrayal behind us. At times, such as when it involves a relationship betrayal, that may be too hard to manage. However, it doesn't mean you can't offer forgiveness within your own heart, even if you can't trust the person not to hurt you again. Do not rush to equate forgiveness with trust and steer clear of those who immediately ask for your forgiveness as well as your trust again after a betrayal. Those are the people who may seek to hurt you once again, because they have learned how easy it is. They must earn your trust.

Forgiveness is beneficial to you, as the person who has been betrayed because it offers you a chance to truly lay to rest your sorrowful feelings and inner pain about the damaging experience of being betrayed. It is not mandated anywhere that you must give over your blind trust again, to anyone. Think of it in terms of a tragic event from history; we learn from the past lest we are doomed to repeat it. And, unless you forgive, in your own heart, you can never look back on the betrayal without a great deal of anger. Where there is anger, there is clouded judgment and consequently, no room for learning and growth. Forgiveness is there to soothe the soul, not to force you to remain in a betraying relationship. When you can learn not only to recognize different types of betrayal, but also to forgive them, it is only then that you can begin to learn from your experiences and protect your heart. So, as you continue to heal, try and keep the concepts of forgiveness and betrayal linked together in your mind and in your heart. It will allow you freedom in the depths of your own personal heart and mind.

In time you will get over the betrayal, with forgiveness in your heart, with your head held high and full of integrity, and with a cool, collected approach to handling the situation. To rise above all the drama that comes along with betrayal is the real challenge. If you can do that, you can continue on with your life and chances are you will not be hurt again. The choice is always there, and the choice is always yours. Choose your friends and lovers wisely, keep your co-worker relationships professional yet distant, and love your siblings in spite of their faults and drama. Be the bigger person and you will never be the betrayer.

Step 6

Cope With the Loss of a Loved One

Experiencing the death of a loved one is never easy, but it is something we will all experience. Whether it happens suddenly in an accident or our loved one has had a long fight with cancer and we've had several weeks or months to prepare for it, it is one of the toughest things we have to deal with as humans. When we love someone, letting go can be the hardest thing imaginable and at times it may seem like we are not going to make it through.

No matter how tough a person is emotionally, they can and should expect to go through the grieving process. Being sad and hurting is a natural expression of how we feel. The good news is that your loved one can and will live on in your memories, and those are available anytime you need. They may seem hurtful to remember in the beginning, but over time, they are what will give you the energy to go on and the love to continue. Perhaps Thomas Campbell said it best, "To live in the hearts we leave behind is not to die."

Stages of Grieving

According to WebMD, there are five stages of the grieving process. They are: denial, bargaining, depression, anger, and acceptance. Denial can include feelings of shock and numbness, and according to the website, "Numbness is a normal reaction to a death or loss and should never be confused with not caring." Over time, these feelings will fade and many people find comfort in helping to plan the funeral and burial, notifying relatives, and even helping to go over important papers, such as wills. At this point in time, keeping busy can help to put the focus on something else, giving you the mental break you may desperately need. Try not to make life changing decisions during this time.

Bargaining takes on the form of thinking of ways you could have prevented the death of your loved one. Thinking things such as, *What if I hadn't asked them to go to the store for me? They never would have gotten into that car crash!* This is an important stage to get through, for anyone feeling guilt over the death. Thinking this way can cause years of pain and grief, all of which are unfounded. For example, if a person had asked someone to go to the store for them, they wouldn't have knowingly sent them if they had expected anything bad to happen. They are called accidents for a reason, and there is no need to feel guilt over it. You could literally take any situation and convince yourself you somehow influenced it, and in some cases that may be true. However, directly blaming yourself doesn't do any good, nor does it bring back your loved one. This stage can be hard for some people, but it is an important stage to work through.

Depression is a common feeling for anyone who has recently lost a loved one. There are a lot of different signs and symptoms that people can display or feel, although many people experience one or more of the following: a change in appetite, feeling tired or being unable to sleep, nightmares, chronic fatigue, crying (sometimes uncontrollably), and anxiety. These are all normal things a person can experience and they are a natural part of the grieving process. Over time, they will subside and may turn into the next stage, anger.

Anger is the next process most people go through and it comes out of a feeling of not being able to do anything to stop the death. It can resemble the bargaining stage in that people question what they might have done differently. The anger can be projected onto the person who caused the accident, including your loved one, doctors who were unable to save them, or even God. These feeling are normal and wanting to blame someone is just a way of dealing with losing your loved one. As the anger starts to fade, the final stage of acceptance is ushered in.

Acceptance is often when the hurting and grieving begins to slow down or stop. This doesn't mean you don't still miss your loved one, you've just accepted they are gone and there is nothing you can do about it. You recognize you'll have memories and cherish the time you had with them, but you are ready to get your own life back together.

It's important to note that although these five stages typically happen in order, there can often be a 'two steps forward, one step back' type of cycle. You may be feeling angry and then go back to the bargaining stage or even back to depression. This is normal for many people and isn't anything to be concerned about. There is also no set time frame for any of the stages to happen. Some people grieve hard and withdraw into themselves and complete the cycle faster than others. Other people can take several years to complete the process. There is no one way that is better or 'right' and it is just an individual process that everyone goes through on their own.

Helping Children Deal with Death

It's important that you talk to children when there is a death in the family. When my father died, I was twelve years old. I felt hurt, confused, and lonely. The visitors that came to the house consoled my mother. They talked and cared for her and the children were sort of left alone. I am sure my mother was devastated to lose her husband and become the sole caretaker of eight children. Don't forget the children when there is a death in the family. They are in pain, too.

Depending on the age of the child, they can grieve differently. Many younger children have a difficult time understanding the concept of death, and even if you explain it thoroughly, they may still think the person is coming back at some point. This is normal and nothing to be worried about. What is important is to answer their questions as best you can, and even if you can't, this is a good time to reinforce your beliefs, whatever they may be.

Children aren't always able to express their feelings the same as adults, because they don't have the vocabulary yet. They can express a variety of behaviors though that can lead you to understanding their pain. According to Parents magazine, these behaviors can include: fighting, denial, mood swing, self-blame, fear of being alone, stomach aches, headaches, trouble sleeping, regression to earlier childhood behaviors, and even issues at school or a 'void' of feelings.

With children, it is always important to let them express their feelings. If they don't want to talk, there are other ways to get them to speak up. Playing quietly next to them can often give them room to speak up and sitting next to them while they draw is another good way to get them to open up. Sometimes it may help if you open up and then give them space to think about their own feelings before talking. Many children also respond to doing something positive in memory of their loved one, such as planting a tree or garden or drawing a special picture. As long as you do it in memory of their loved one, they will appreciate being able to put forth effort in memory of them.

Older children will grieve much like adults, but may exhibit some signs of regressive behavior. With older kids, it's important to keep an eye on them to be sure they aren't overly depressed. While depression is normal, older children may not have the skills to cope so it is important to make sure they are dealing with the death in a normal manner, and if not, seek professional help for them.

Ways to Celebrate Your Loved One's Life in Their Honor

Losing someone you love is hard, but certain things can help to make it easier. Just like with children, doing something positive can help to make you feel better. Children associate things such as planting a tree or garden with remembering their loved one, and adults can benefit from the same type of symbolism. If the family has the means, they can donate to a cause near and dear to their loved one's heart or they could 'buy' a star and name it after their loved one.

Many zoos, museums, and parks allow people to donate money for a memorial bench. Maybe your loved one enjoyed the lions at the zoo. What better way than to give others a place to rest and watch these majestic animals than by buying seating with a special plaque? If they had a favorite clothing item or T-shirt collection, you can find individuals who will sew them into a pattern for a blanket. There are also memory quilts which you can get knitted in their favorite colors.

This is a project more than one person can get involved in and depending on your loved ones likes and interests, you can think up the perfect thing to remember them with. This can help the healing process to complete, and can be a wonderful way to remember them. It is important to remember that your love will never die, and there are ways to keep the special memories alive.

When Grief Turns into Depression

The grieving process includes depression, but there is a point when depression can last too long and take on a life of its own. According to the National Institute of Health, there are certain signs and symptoms you should look for if you're concerned you or a family member has let the grieving turn into something else. These feelings can include feeling sad or empty, feeling hopeless, irritable, anxious, and even guilty.

People suffering from depression can also lose interest in activities they normally love, exhibit excessive tiredness, have difficulty concentrating and remembering details, sleep much more or much less than normal, eat much more or much less than normal, have aches and pains, and even think about or try suicide. If you suspect this, it is time to get professional help.

Temporary help for serious depression can mean talking with a psychologist, lifestyle changes, or a combination of both of them. When you're suffering from serious depression, it is imperative to get help immediately once you recognize it. The sooner you get help, the sooner you'll be back to feeling your normal self. This doesn't mean you'll not feel sad about losing someone you loved dearly, it just means you'll be able to cope. Many people suffering from severe depression are unable to go to work and can't function as they should. The sooner you can get back to a normal balance in your life, the sooner you'll be able to deal with the death and process your feelings.

The following accounts are from people who have lost loved ones.

Mary's son committed suicide and she was devastated. Her family was not supportive and she felt so alone.

Taj's close friend died unexpectedly from unknown causes and she was having a hard time accepting her death. She would never be able to talk to her again. Good friends are hard to find. She lived in a big city and she was searching for help to help her cope.

Laura's husband died after 32 years of marriage. She felt lost so she sat down and started writing about their life. After 10 hours of writing she felt better. It really helped putting her thoughts down on paper.

Helen lost her husband to cancer. For 30 years, he always took care of day to day things. She's scared because she doesn't know what to do. Her one consolation is that she believes she will see him again because he believed in God.

Wilhemina lost her husband after 26 years to colon cancer. She finds it hard to cope without him. They made all decisions and did everything together. Now there is no one to share her days and nights with. She doesn't know how to manage her days and is afraid that she may be going into depression.

Jacqueline lost her husband still doesn't feel it is real. She has no friends around her because they had moved two years prior to his death. She feels isolated and lonely. She feels like she is stuck in limbo and can't seem to get on with her life. She is financially ruined because unknown to her, her husband had cashed out his life insurance several years prior to his death. She is devastated.

Talulah is a 54 year old woman who has lost two sons. One was murdered in the neighborhood and one was killed in a car accident. Somehow she managed to get through with the love and support of her husband and her remaining children as well as her friends. Her husband was a truck driver and they traveled together for nearly 10 years. He suddenly died of a heart attack. Since then, her life has been so lonely and empty she doesn't want to go on. Her health has gone downhill. She cries at the drop of a hat. She has migraine headaches and can't get rid of them. She doesn't know how to go on living without him. Life without him is horrible. Others say, "Time will heal" and "He's in a better place". That makes her so angry! How does a person live on day after day with so much pain?

Madge lost her husband, best friend and the pain is unbearable and she doesn't see it getting any better. When people ask, "How are you feeling?" No one will ever understand unless they walk in her shoes. Life just has no meaning without him. People make her angry when they say he is in a better place because to her there is no better place than being together. She doesn't feel like she is living anymore, just managing to get by each day.

Marlo is having a very hard time dealing with the death of her fiancé. They were to get married but he died in an accident 20 days before. She cries all the time. They have a son together. Her fiancé was also her best friend. She knows she has to be strong for their son. She tries to keep as busy as possible but she can't wait to fall asleep so she doesn't have to think anymore. She doesn't want to do anything and her friends don't understand. She feels alone, hurt, scared, confused, and distraught.

Octavia lost her husband of 13 years. It was unexpected. She took him to the hospital and he died two weeks later. She felt lost and betrayed by his doctor and really sad because there was so much she didn't get to say to him before he passed. It hits hard at different times. She thinks she can deal with it but she just falls apart. She says that she needs help.

Norm was very emotional when he said that most information about the loss of a loved one was geared towards women and he thought that was unfair. Men do have feelings and experience the same emotions when losing a loved one.

It's sometimes difficult to get men to talk about their pain after losing a loved one. If you know a male friend or family member that has lost a loved one, let them know that you are there for them if they want to talk. Don't force the conversation.

I lost one son when he was two years old. He died from a congenital heart defect. Today, I think that particular condition is corrected while baby is in the womb. I just remember a sadness that lingered for a long time. I lost another son to murder. It is a parent's hope that they will not bury their children. At that time of his death, I had a profound sadness; but I knew from past experience that God would supply the grace that

I needed to get through it. Now, I enjoy precious memories.

After a loss, you need support to help you heal. After the burial of your loved one, people stop calling and visiting and you go back to your daily activities and sometimes push that pain aside. Many people start to drink, take drugs, eat too much…do anything to keep that pain buried. Some people never really go through the healing process referenced in the above paragraphs. Because of social networks, it is easy to reach out and find someone or a group to share your loss and pain. When you know someone has experienced the same pain, it is more comforting to hear from them. Reach out for help if you think you need it.

Suggestions for dealing with your grief:

- Accept that you will have a wide range of feelings

- Know that everyone's experience is different

- Take care of yourself, eat nourishing food, try to get plenty of rest

- Don't feel guilty when you experience happiness on some days

- Lean on your faith that this, too, shall pass

- Join a support group

- It may take some time but be patient and allow yourself to embrace life again

- Get professional help if needed

A famous gravestone in Ireland simply says, "Death leaves a heartache no one can heal, love leaves a memory no one can steal." The pain of losing a loved one might not ever really end, but you will have special memories to last the rest of your lifetime. It's up to you to honor your loved one in a way you see fit, and in a way that helps heal your heart.

Step 7

Be Persistent

The Merriam-Webster dictionary defines the word persistent as *continuing to do something or to try to do something even though it is difficult or other people want you to stop and continuing beyond the usual, expected, or normal time: not stopping or going away.* So whether you're looking to be successful in accomplishing a personal or professional goal, it's important to consider the value of persistence in any endeavor you might take on.

If you look close enough, there are examples of persistence all around, and how it pays off. From the time we're just babies we have periods where persistence is necessary and we have understood that it takes hard work and repeatedly doing the same thing to get what we want. Just look at a baby lying in a crib who wants to turn himself over for the first time. The baby will repeatedly try and push over time and again until he finally gets it. The baby may get frustrated before he does get it, but it doesn't stop him from continually trying. Once he is finally able to turn over, he realizes it *is* within his power to do it all by himself. There may be a few stumbles the next few times he tries, but eventually it happens in a routine fashion and he's got it down pat. Then, the baby is on to learning a new thing to do, going through the process of trial and error all over again.

There are numerous examples of when being persistent has paid off in the adult world as well. Take for example J.K. Rowling, the author of the extremely popular *Harry Potter* series. Although she is one of the wealthiest women in the world, it took a lot of hard work and dedication to get to where she is now, which is worth over an estimated $1 billion. She had been in the middle of many personal setbacks when writing her first book, *Harry Potter and the Sorcerer's Stone*. From getting divorced, having her mother die, and becoming dependent on the welfare system, she had her share of obstacles. Then, when she finished the first book, it was turned down by 12 publishers. The publisher who finally did print the first book told her that although his company would publish it, she should probably consider getting a day job since she wouldn't likely make much money from it.

Another good example of when being persistent has paid off is with Milton Hershey. Milton dropped out of school at a young age to work as an apprentice for a printer. After being fired, he became an apprentice for a candy maker and found his real passion. After four years, he set out on his own and started a string of unsuccessful companies, until he started the Lancaster Caramel Company. Although the company was successful he wasn't satisfied and felt that his future lay in chocolate, which up to that point wasn't widely available in the U.S. Once he started, there was no stopping him. What had been a vision turned into one of the top confectioner companies in the U.S.

One of the most inspiring stories of persistence lies in the history books with Abraham Lincoln. He came from a poor farming family and lost his mother when he was just nine years old. Even through tough times, he had a great work ethic and continued to plow through life with persistence and hard work, ultimately reaching the top. Although he was always interested in politics and ran for a variety of offices throughout his life, he lost as often as he won, but getting beat out by other candidates never stopped him. His views at the time went against what a lot of people believed, but he held tight to his convictions and eventually won the presidency in 1860 and changed the course of America.

Although these are all examples of famous people who most may be familiar with, there are just as many stories of everyday people accomplishing goals or overcoming obstacles due to their persistence. One excellent example of this is with Becky Guinn of Alabama. She had been an art teacher at the local high school for years when she had a severe reaction to a new medication she was taking. It cost her both her hands and feet. Most artists might have given up at that point, but not Becky. With an incredible attitude and a lot of persistence, she returned to teaching less than a week after getting her prosthetic arms. She went from shaky handwriting after the surgery to being able to create some of the best artwork she's ever done. She obviously didn't accomplish this by happenstance one day, but rather by repeated hard work and determination. She is now back to teaching and doing what she loves best, almost as if the accident had never happened. She is also a great inspiration to her students.

Why be Persistent?

When anyone takes on the mentality of being persistent to accomplish something, it can change their whole outlook on life. Knowing what you want, and being ready to get it, are key components that can guide you to successfully being persistent in your pursuit. Take for example a new job you want to obtain. If you repeatedly do what it takes to get that job, whether it is on the job training, going back to school, or just rising up the corporate ladder one step at a time, you should eventually get what you want when you're determined and have taken the time to do what's needed.

There are always those people who will try something once and give up. Maybe they want a new job and apply for it, but when they're not chosen they decide to just give up, thinking *I'll never get it anyway.* This is the perfect example of when persistence could pay off. Things we want are rarely just given to us; it takes work and determination to get it. When you want something so badly you can envision it, such as yourself in that job, it can take on a whole new life of its own.

There are numerous ways to be persistent in all areas of life. From improving your relationships to getting out of debt, there's really no limit to what perseverance can do for you. Being persistent also shows dedication in getting the best life has to offer. When we are complacent and willing to take what's given us, we can often lose our zest for life. When we have goals and are ready to tackle them head on, it can often change a person's mindset. They are able to focus on goals and live life with a renewed enthusiasm. Improving life in any area can be accomplished with persistence, whether it's used for repairing bad credit, seeking a new job or any other number of things. Once the goal has been accomplished, the act of persevering until reaching the goal can be transferred to a new goal. There can also be multiple goals at once.

The good thing about it is when you accomplish something you've gone after, it opens your eyes to the many other possibilities that are out there. You become more dedicated and determined in all areas of your life. This is also a great trait to pass on to children if you have them. Some kids have little patience for working towards goals, so teaching them about persistence can serve them well all their lives.

Determine Your Goal

Persistence can be applied to all types of goals ranging from short term to long term. However, short term to long term goals can be accomplished using the same tactics and there is a process to help you in being persistent when wanting to accomplish something. First, it's important to know precisely what your goal is. If you think you want to lose weight, some people would say that is really just a dream. When you determine exactly how much weight you want to lose and how you want to lose the extra weight, it becomes a goal. You have defined *exactly* what you want. Once you have the specific goal you can then determine the actions you need to take to reach that goal.

To start, it works best to have a plan. For example, if your goal is to lose weight you'll want to determine how much you want to lose each week until you reach your goal. You'll have to decide how you want to lose the weight, such as by dieting, eating smaller meals more frequently to increase your metabolism, and/or working out. Once you've got your plan in place, it's important to visualize what you will feel like once you've reached your goal.

Visualization techniques have been around for years, and are popular with some very successful athletes. Even the popular American author Napoleon Hill once said, "Whatever your mind can conceive and believe, it can achieve." If you really want something but can't see it coming to fruition, it may be elusive to you no matter how hard you work. When you are persistent and visualize your goals, you have the exact ingredients you need to reach them.

After you've determined your plan and begun to visualize it, it's time to take action. Follow any steps you've outlined and if you come across a hurdle, look at it as an obstacle in which you can gain more information or consider it a test to pass before you can really get what you want. Some successful people look at obstacles as learning points or what not to do the next time around. Dale Carnegie, a writer and pioneer in the personal development industry once said, "Most of the important things in the world have been accomplished by people who have kept on trying when there seemed to be no hope at all." If this is indeed the case, it makes it even more imperative to follow your goals through to completion with persistence and dedication. When talking about his invention of the light bulb and how many tries it took him, Thomas Edison said, "I have not failed. I've just found 10,000 ways that won't work." There probably aren't too many people who have tried something that many times without having gotten what they were ultimately working towards, although Mr. Edison proved that persistence pays off, and every time we turn on a light switch we can thank him for it.

Change Your Habits

Habits can be good or bad, depending on what they are. There is conflicting information about how long it takes to get into or break out of a habit, although most people agree it lies within a time frame of 30 to 60 days. People will vary in their timeframe for changing a habit depending on their personality or how long they may have had a habit as well as other factors. But knowing it can be done can be liberating, especially when it comes to being persistent. Aristotle said, "We are what we repeatedly do. Excellence, then, is not an act, but a habit." So if new habits are aligned with goals, there is a highly likely chance that persistence in changing our habits will pay off in obtaining goals.

Teachers of young students have often realized the importance of teaching persistence. When kids are given a variety of new skills to learn in the classroom, such as math problems, there is bound to be a learning curve for many of them. Good teachers recognize this and encourage persistence instead of just telling the student the answer or having them immediately try it another way. There is intrinsic value in persistence and learning this early on is conducive to continuing the practice into adulthood.

However, there are also children who have been doted on a good portion of their lives and will find being persistent to be much more difficult later on in life. The good news is that anyone can learn to be persistent. In addition to writing out goals and how you plan to achieve them, many people find that when they actually write the reason down why they want to accomplish something it gives them more determination.

Say, for example, a husband and wife have found themselves in debt. This can cause friction between the couple and affect other aspects of their life as well, such as their health from all the stress. They may want and know they need to get out of debt, but without a real plan or written reasons why they want this, it may be more elusive. If they write down a plan and why it's important for them to get out of debt, with persistence they are much more likely to reach their goal of being debt free.

The reasons for wanting the goal of being debt free could vary from becoming stress free to feeling more in control to setting a good example for their children to follow. When the reason is clear, along with the goal and the plan, persistence will pay off whether it's paying down debt, losing weight, obtaining a coveted new job, or any variety of other goals a person may have.

Are You Willing to Work and Do You Want it Bad Enough?

Lee Iacocca, the famous American businessman, was known for some of his great quotes. This is what he said on this subject, "You've got to say, "I think that if I keep working at this and want it badly enough I can have it." It's called perseverance." Although it may seem obvious to say anyone has to work to get to their goals, it is a trait that can be lacking in some people. With the hectic lives we lead today, sometimes the simplest of things can seem elusive, such as the concept of persistence. There are of course those who have been told somewhere along the way they can't do something. If this is the case, it's important to remember that you are in control and someone else's opinion is just that, an opinion.

If you haven't really tried to reach any goals for a while and want to try it, start with something small. Maybe losing three pounds or saving $100 for a rainy day. When you start small and begin to change your habits, you will reach your goal. Then, you can begin to set even larger goals and the skills and dedication you learned while reaching your smaller goals will kick in. When you decide to try persistence for yourself in any area of life, it can easily transfer to all areas of your life.

One of the biggest boosts you can give yourself is to believe in yourself. It's also important to remember that challenges often come when we are pursuing goals, but with challenges also come greater rewards and an even greater feeling of accomplishment when the goal is finally reached. In addition to creating goals it's important to remember how persistence has paid off for many people, and it can for you, too. When you have a mission and understand the path it takes to reach your destination, you will get there through persistence, just like the many people who have done it before.

Above all, remember that the persona you really need costs nothing. Cars, homes, friends, and money will come and go. Persistence, compassion, respect for yourself and others can last a lifetime and make you feel good.

When you enhance your self-esteem, communicate clearly, manage conflict, exhibit integrity, deal with betrayal, cope with the loss of a loved one and be persistent in each of these endeavors, you will improve your personal and interpersonal skills.

> ***"To be yourself in a world that is constantly trying to make you something else is the greatest accomplishment."***
>
> **—EMERSON**

Bonus Article

THE HABIT OF HAPPINESS

By O. S. Marden

The utmost happiness must always come from using the best in us. When you find happiness in anything but useful work, you'll be the first person to make the discovery. If you take an inventory of yourself at the very beginning of your career, you will find that you think you are going to find happiness in possessions or in circumstances.

Most people think they are going to find the major part of their happiness in money, what money will buy or what it will give them in the way of power, influence, comforts, and luxuries. They think they are going to find a great deal of their happiness in marriage. How quickly they find that the greatest happiness they will ever know is that which must be limited to their own capacity for enjoyment. Their happiness cannot come from anything outside of them but must be developed from within.

Many people believe they are going to find much of their happiness in books, travel, leisure, and freedom from the thousand and one anxieties, cares, and worries of business; but the moment they get in the position where they thought they would have freedom, many other things come up in their minds and cut off much of the expected joy. When they get money and leisure they often find that they are growing selfish, which cuts off a lot of their happiness.

Idleness is the last place to look for happiness. Idleness is like a stagnant pool. The moment the water ceases to flow, to work, to do something, all sorts of vermin and hideous creatures develop in it. It becomes stagnant and unhealthy giving out murkiness and repulsive odors. In the same way, work is the only thing that will keep the individual healthy, wholesome, and clean. An idle brain very quickly breeds impurities.

The married man quickly learns that his family's happiness depends upon what he contributes to the partnership that he cannot take out a great deal without putting a great deal in. Selfishness always reaps a mean, shameful harvest. It is only the generous giver who gets much. Selfishness is always a fatal blighter, blaster, and disappointer. We must give to get, we must be great before we can get great enjoyment; great in our motive, grand in our endeavor, and sublime in our ideas.

It is rare for a bad person to be truly happy; just as rare as it would be for one to be comfortable while lying on a bed of nettles which are constantly pricking him. Can a person be really happy without being good, clean, honest, and true? This does not mean that a person is happy because he does not smoke, drink, gamble, use profane language or does not do other vicious things. Some of the meanest, narrowest, most contemptible people in the world do none of these things but they are uncharitable, jealous, envious, and revengeful. They stab you in the back, slander you, and cheat you. They may be cunning, underhanded, and yet have a fairly good standing in the church.

No person can be really happy who has a small, narrow, bigoted, uncharitable mind or disposition. Generosity, charity, and kindness are absolutely essential to real happiness. Deceitful people cannot be happy; they cannot respect themselves because they inwardly despise themselves for deceiving people. A person must be open minded, transparent, and simple, in order to be really happy. A person who is always covering up something, trying to keep things from you, misleading you, and deceiving you, cannot get away from self-reproach, and therefore cannot be really happy.

The liar is never really happy. He is always on pins and needles for fear his deceit may betray him.

He never feels safe. Dishonesty in all its phases is fatal to happiness, for no dishonest person can get his self-approval. Without this, no happiness is possible.

Before you can be really happy, you must be able to look back upon a well-spent past, a conscientious, unselfish past. If not, you will be haunted by demons which will destroy your happiness. If you have been mean and selfish, greedy and dishonest with your associates and relationships, all sorts of horrible things will rise out of your money pile to terrify and to make your happiness impossible.

In other words, happiness is merely a result of the life work. It will partake of the exact quality of the motive which you have put into your life work. If these motives have been selfish, greedy, and grasping, or if cunning and dishonesty have dominated in your career, your happiness will be marred accordingly.

You cannot complain of your happiness, because it is your own child, the product of your own brain, your own effort. It has been made up of your motives, tinted by your life aim. It corresponds exactly to the cause which produced it.

There is the greatest difference in the world between the happiness which comes from a sweet, beautiful, unselfish, helpful, sympathetic, industrious, honorable career, and the mean satisfaction which may grow to be a part of your marked self if you have lived a selfish, grasping life.

What we call happiness is the harvest from our life sowing, our habitual thought-sowing, and deed-doing. If we have sown selfish, envious, jealous, revengeful, hateful seeds, greedy, and grasping seeds, we cannot expect a golden happiness harvest like that which comes from a clean, unselfish, and helpful sowing.

If our harvest is full of the rank, poisonous weeds of jealousy, envy, dishonesty, cunning, and cruelty, we have no one to blame but ourselves, for we sowed the seed which produced that sort of a harvest.

Somehow some people have an entirely wrong idea of what real happiness is. They seem to think it can be bought, had by influence, and purchased by money. They believe that if they have money they can get that wonderful, mysterious thing which they call happiness.

But happiness is a natural, faithful harvest from our sowing. It would be as impossible for selfish seed, greed seed to produce a harvest of contentment, genuine satisfaction, real joy, as for thistle seeds to produce a harvest of wheat or corn.

Whatever the quality of your enjoyment or happiness may be, you have patterned it by your life motive by the spirit in which you have worked, and by the principles which have motivated you.

Many of us face all sorts of hideous, poisonous weeds, but they are all the legitimate product of our sowing. No one can rob us of our harvest or change it very much. Every thought, act, and motive, whether secret or public, is a seed which no power on earth can prevent going to its harvest of beauty or ugliness, honor or shame. Most people have an idea that happiness is something that can be manufactured. They do not realize that it can no more be manufactured than wheat or corn can be manufactured. It must be grown, and the harvest will be like the seed.

Make up your mind at the very beginning of your career that whatever comes to you in life, that whether you succeed or fail, whether you have this or that, there is one thing you will have, and that is a happy, contented mind, and you will extract your happiness as you go along. You will not take the chances of picking up or developing the happy habit after you get rich, for then it may be too late.

Most people postpone their enjoyment until they are disappointed to find the power of enjoyment has largely gone by and that even if they had the means they could not get anything like as much real happiness out of it as they could have gotten as they went along when they were younger. Take no chances with your happiness, or the sort of a life that can produce it; whatever else you risk, do not risk this. Early form the happy habit, the habit of enjoyment every day, no matter what comes or does not come to you during the day. No matter how unpleasant or disagreeable your situation is, pick out crumbs of comfort.

I know a man who, although poor, can manage to get more comfort out of a real tough, discouraging situation than anyone else I have ever seen. I have often seen him when he did not have a dollar to his name, with a family to support; yet he was always buoyant, happy, and cheerful. He would even make fun out of an embarrassing situation… see something ludicrous in his extreme poverty.

There have never been such conflicting estimates, such varying ideas, regarding any state of human condition as to what constitutes happiness. Many people think that it is purchasable with money, but many of the most restless, discontented, unhappy people in the world are rich. They have the means of purchasing what they *thought* would produce happiness, but the real thing escapes them. On the other hand, some of the poorest people in the world are happy. The fact is that there is no possible way of cornering or purchasing happiness for it is absolutely beyond the reach of money. It is true; we can purchase a few comforts and immunities from some annoyances and worries with money which we cannot get without it. On the other hand, the great majority of people who have inherited money are sometimes injured by it, because it often stops their own development by taking away the motive for self-effort and self-reliance.

When people get money they often stop growing because they depend upon the money instead of relying upon their own inherent resources. It could be said that rich people suffer from their indulgences more than poor ones suffer from their hardships.

If people try to seek happiness through the avenue of leisure they soon find that an idle brain is one of the most dangerous things in the world—nothing deteriorates faster. The mind was made for continual strong action, systematic, vigorous exercise, and this is possible only when some dominating aim and a great life purpose leads the way.

No person can be really healthful whose mind is not usefully and continually active. Nature brings a wonderful compensatory power to those who are crippled or sick or otherwise disabled from working, but there is no compensation for idleness in those who are able to work. Nature only gives us the use of faculties we employ. "Use or lose" is her motto, and when we cease to use a faculty or function it is gradually taken away from us, gradually shrivels and atrophies.

There is no satisfaction like that which comes from the steady, persistent, honest, conscientious pursuit of a good plan. There are a multitude of evidences in man's very structure that his marvelous mechanism was intended for action, for constant exercise, and that idleness and stagnation always mean deterioration and death of control. No man can remain idle without shrinking, shriveling, constantly becoming a less efficient man; for he can keep up only those faculties and powers which he constantly uses. Nature puts her ban of deterioration and loss of power upon idleness. Without some means of work, mental health is impossible and without health the fullest happiness is impossible.

It has been said that happiness is the most misleading thing that man pursues. Yet, why should it be a blind search? If we were to stop the first hundred people we meet on the street and ask them what in their experience has given them the most happiness, probably the answer of no two would be alike.

How interesting and instructive it would be to give a thousand dollars to each of these hundred people, and without their knowing it, follow them and see what they would do with the money,— what it would mean to them.

To some poor youth hungry for an education, with no opportunity to gain it, this money would go toward a college education. Another would see in his money help for aged parents. To another this money would suggest all sorts of indulgence. Some would see books and leisure for self-improvement, or perhaps a trip abroad.

We all wear different colored glasses and no two see life with the same tint.

Some find their present happiness in common indulgence; others in a quiet nook with a book. Some find their greatest happiness in friends and social gatherings. Others seek happiness in wandering from place to place— always thinking that the greatest enjoyment is in another day, another place, a little further on, in the next room, tomorrow, or in another country.

To many people, happiness is never where they are, but almost anywhere else.

Most people lose sight of the simplicity of happiness. They look for it in big, complicated things. Real happiness is perfectly simple. In fact, it is incompatible with complexity. Simplicity is its very essence.

There is a successful young man who is trying very hard to be happy, but he takes such a complicated, strenuous view of everything that his happiness is always soaring from him. He drives everything so fiercely; his life is so vigorous and so complicated that happiness cannot find a home with him very long. Nor does he understand why. He has money, health; but he always has that restless far-away, absent-minded gaze into something beyond, and I do not think he is ever really very happy. His whole manner of living is extremely complex. He does not seem to know where to find happiness. He has evidently mistaken the very nature of happiness. He thinks it consists in making a great show, having great possessions, doing things which attract a great deal of attention; but *happiness would be strangled, suffocated in such an environment.* The essentials of real happiness are few, simple, and close at hand.

Happiness is made up of very simple ingredients. It flees from the complex life. It evades pomp and show. The heart would starve amid the greatest luxuries. Simple joys and the treasures of the heart and mind make happiness. Happiness has very little to do with material things. It is a mental state of mind. Real permanent happiness cannot be found in mere temporary things, because its roots reach way down into eternal principles. One of the most pathetic pictures in society is the many men and women searching the world over for happiness, as though it existed in things rather than in a state of mind.

The people who have spent years and a fortune trying to find it look as hungry and as lean of contentment and all that makes life desirable as when they started out. Chasing happiness all over the world is about as silly a business as any human being ever engaged in, for it was never found by any pursuer. Yet happiness is the simplest thing in the world. It is found in many a home with carpetless floors and pictureless walls. It does not recognize rank, station, color, nor does it recognize wealth. It only demands that it live with a contented mind and pure heart. It will not live with ostentation; it flees from pretense; it loves the simple life; it insists upon a sweet, healthful and natural environment.

Real happiness flees from the things that pass away; it abides only in principle and permanency. I have never seen a person who has lived a grasping, greedy, money-chasing life, who was not disappointed at what money has given him for his trouble. It is only in giving and helping that we find our mission. Everywhere we go we see people who are disappointed, annoyed, and shocked to find that what they thought would be the angel of happiness turned out to be only a ghost.

All the misery and the crime of the world rest upon the failure of human beings to understand the principle that *no man can really be happy until he harmonizes with the best thing in him, with the divine, and not with the brute.* No one can be happy who tries to harmonize his life with his animal instincts. *The God (the good) in him is the only possible thing that can make him happy.*

Real happiness cannot be bribed by anything sordid or low. Nothing mean or unworthy appeals to it. There is no affinity between them. Founded upon principle, it is as scientific as the laws of mathematics, and he who works his problem correctly will get the happiness answer.

It does not matter that the great majority of the human race believes there is some other way of reaching the happiness goal. The fact that they are discontented, restless, and unhappy shows that they are not working their problem scientifically.

The very essence of happiness is honesty, sincerity, and truthfulness. It is just as impossible for a person to reach the normal state of harmony while he is practicing selfish, grasping methods, as it is to produce harmony in an orchestra with instruments that are all jangled and out of tune. To be happy, we must be in tune with the infinite within us and in harmony with our better selves. There is no way to get around it.

There is no tonic like that which comes from doing things worthwhile. There is no happiness like that which comes from doing our level best every day and everywhere. There is no satisfaction like that which comes from stamping superiority and putting our royal trademark upon everything which goes through our hands.

Recently a rich young man was asked why he did not work. "I do not have to," he said. "Do not have to" has ruined more young men than almost anything else. The fact is, Nature never made any provision for the idle man. Vigorous activity is the law of life; it is the saving grace, the only thing that can keep a human being from retrograding. Activity along the line of one's highest ambition is the normal state of man, and he who tries to evade it pays the penalty in deterioration of ability and loss of competence. Do not flatter yourself that you can be really happy unless you are useful. Happiness and usefulness were born twins. To separate them is fatal.

It is as impossible for a human being to be happy who is habitually idle as it is for a fine chronometer to be normal when not running. The highest happiness is the feeling of wellbeing which comes to one who is actively working doing what he was made to do. The practical fulfilling of the life purpose is to man what the actual running and keeping time are to the watch. Without action both are meaningless.

Man was made to do things. Nothing else can take the place of achievement in his life. Real happiness without achievement of some worthy aim is unthinkable. One of the greatest satisfactions in this world is the feeling of improvement, growth, and stretching upward and onward.

Happiness is incompatible with stagnation. A man must feel his expanding power lifting, tugging away at a lofty purpose, or he will miss the joy of living. The discords, the bickering, the divorces, the breaking up of rich homes, and the resorting to all sorts of silly devices by many rich people in their pursuit of happiness, prove that it does not dwell with them; that happiness does not abide with low ideals, with selfishness, idleness, and discord. It is a friend of harmony, of truth, of beauty, of affection, of simplicity. Many people have made fortunes, but have destroyed their capacity for enjoyment in the process. How often we hear the remark, "He has the money, but cannot enjoy it."

The greatest delusion that a man can have is that he can spend the best years of his life coining all of his energies into dollars, neglecting his home, sacrificing friendships, self-improvement, and everything else that is really worthwhile, for money, and yet find happiness at the end! The happiness habit is just as necessary to our best welfare as the work habit, or the honesty or square-dealing habit. Are you happy?

About the Author

Marie McCurley, born and raised in a suburb of Chicago, has retired from the traditional world or work and now operates her own publishing company. Her career experiences consist of, but are not limited to, published author, employee development specialist, interpersonal skills trainer, director of a not for profit organization, licensed real estate salesperson, a community college instructor, and a small business owner.

Marie owned and operated Professional Excellence (an interpersonal skills training service) and 1st Class Virtual Administrative Assistance for five years. Marie published her first book, The Easy Way to Plan a Church Conference in 2000 and published a Revised Edition in 2013.

In 2001 Marie received the William N. Frayser Award of Excellence-Attaining Great Heights in Literary Acclaim, Female Business Ownership, and Social Service.

Marie has three children, seven grandchildren, and two great grandchildren. She enjoys writing, dancing, and playing her digital piano. She looks forward to writing more books.

Bibliography

Active Listening, SkillsYouNeed, Founded in July 2011, UK Web Archive.

Betrayal. http://www.carolthecoach.com/articles/relationships.

Bloodworth, Venice, Key To Yourself (DeVores & Company, Marina Del Ray, CA, 1952).

Bramson, Robert, Coping With Difficult People (Ballantine Books, New York, 1981).

Build-Character-Through-Integrity. http://www.wikihow.com.

Cava, Roberta, Difficult People (Firefly Books, Inc., Buffalo, New York, 1997).

Clemson University, South Carolina. N.p., n.d. Web. 10 Oct. 2013.

Conflict. Merriam-Webster. Merriam-Webster, n.d. Web. 10 Oct. 2013.

Department of Commerce, U.S. Census Bureau Reports Housing Is Top Reason People Moved Between 2009 and 2010. N.p., n.d. Web. 10 Oct. 2013.

Depression. *NIMH RSS*. N.p., n.d. Web. 23 May 2014. <http://www.nimh.nih.gov/health/publications/depression-easy-to-read/index.shtml.

Diehm, William J., Sharpen Your People Skills (Broadman & Holman Publishers, Nashville, TN.

Drew, Naomi. Peaceful Parents, Peaceful Kids: Practical Ways to Create a Calm and Happy Home. New York: Kensington, 2000. Print.

Edmonds Community College: Home. Edmonds Community College: Home. N.p., n.d. Web. 10 Oct. 2013. http://www.edcc.edu/counseling/documents/Conflict.pdfensington Publishing Corp.

Grief & Depression Coping With Denial, Loss, Anger and More." WebMD. WebMD, n.d. Web. 23 May 2014. <http://www.webmd.com/depression/guide/depression-grief.

Helping Kids Cope with Grief." *Parents Magazine*. N.p., n.d. Web. 23 May 2014. <http://www.parents.com/kids/development/behavioral/helping-kids-cope-grief/#page=5.

Hill, Napoleon, Think and Grow Rich, Combined Registry, Chicago, IL, 1960.

Marden, Orison Swett, Pushing to the Front, Success Company, Petersburg, N.Y., 1911.

Munro, Dan. http://addicted2success.com/life/how-why-you-should-live-a-life-of-integrity, September 2013.

Resolving Family Conficts. http://www.clemson.edu/fyd/Assets/Adobe_Acrobat_files/tcct._

Resolving Workplace Conflict", Resolving Workplace Conflict. N.p., n.d. Web. 10 Oct. 2013.\Tennessee, 1996).

Sibling Betrayal and Estrangement in Dysfunctional Families. http://soulpancake.com/conversations/view/79429/ (accessed 2014).

Signs You Lack Integrity. http://careynieuwhof.com 2012/02/5.

www.ingramcontent.com/pod-product-compliance
Lightning Source LLC
Chambersburg PA
CBHW071506040426
42444CB00008B/1525